Transfiguring Life

OTHER BOOKS BY ANDREW D. MAYES

spiritualityadviser.com

Celebrating the Christian Centuries (1999)

Spirituality of Struggle: Pathways to Growth (2002)

Spirituality in Ministerial Formation (2009)

Holy Land? Challenging Questions from the Biblical Landscape (2011)

Beyond the Edge: Spiritual Transitions for Adventurous Souls (2013)

Another Christ: Re-envisioning Ministry (2014)

Learning the Language of the Soul (2016)

Journey to the Centre of the Soul (2017)

Sensing the Divine (2019)

Gateways to the Divine: Transformative Pathways of Prayer from the Holy City of Jerusalem (2020)

Diving for Pearls: Exploring the Depths of Prayer with Isaac the Syrian (2021)

Voices from the Mountains: Forgotten Wisdom for a Hurting World from the Biblical Peaks (2021)

Climate of the Soul: Ecological Spirituality for Anxious Times (2022)

Reforesting the Soul: Meditating with Trees (2022)

Treasure in the Wilderness: Desert Spirituality for Uncertain Times (2023)

Roads of Hurt and Hope: Transformative Journeys in the Holy Land (2024)

Another Christ: Rediscovering Jesus, Francis, and Discipleship Today (2024)

Transfiguring Life

Unleashing the Power of Paradox

ANDREW D. MAYES

RESOURCE *Publications* · Eugene, Oregon

TRANSFIGURING LIFE
Unleashing the Power of Paradox

Copyright © 2025 Andrew D. Mayes. All rights reserved. Except for brief quotations in critical publications or reviews, no part of this book may be reproduced in any manner without prior written permission from the publisher. Write: Permissions, Wipf and Stock Publishers, 199 W. 8th Ave., Suite 3, Eugene, OR 97401.

Resource Publications
An Imprint of Wipf and Stock Publishers
199 W. 8th Ave., Suite 3
Eugene, OR 97401

www.wipfandstock.com

PAPERBACK ISBN: 979-8-3852-4413-3
HARDCOVER ISBN: 979-8-3852-4414-0
EBOOK ISBN: 979-8-3852-4415-7
VERSION NUMBER 04/09/25

Unless otherwise acknowledged, Scripture quotations are from New Revised Standard Version Bible, Copyright © 1989, 1995 National Council of the Churches of Christ in the United States of America. Used by permission. All rights reserved worldwide.

Amplified Bible (AMP/AMPC) © 1954–2015 Lockman Foundation.

Authorized (King James) Version (AKJV/ AV) Cambridge University Press.

The Christian Standard Bible (CSB) © 2017 Holman Bible Publishers.

English Standard Version (ESV) © 2001 Crossway Bibles, Good News Publishers.

The Expanded Bible (EXB) © 2011 Thomas Nelson Inc.

The Jerusalem Bible (JB) © 1966 Darton, Longman and Todd.

The Living Bible (TLB) © 1971 Tyndale House Foundation.

The Message (MSG) © 1993, 2002, 2018 Eugene H. Peterson.

New English Translation (NET) ©1996–2017 Biblical Studies Press.

New American Bible Revised Edition (NABRE) © 2010 Confraternity of Christian Doctrine.

New International Version (NIV) © 1979, 1984, 2011 Biblica, Inc.

New Life Version (NLV) © 1969, 2003 by Barbour Publishing.

New Testament for Everyone (NTFE) © 2011, 2018, 2019 Nicholas Thomas Wright

J. B. Phillips New Testament in Modern English (PHILLIPS) © 1960, 1972 J. B. Phillips.

Revised Standard Version (RSV) © 1946, 1952, 1971 Division of Christian Education of the National Council of the Churches of Christ in the United States of America.

Contents

Images and Credits		vii
Introduction		1
1	Reaching: Between Heaven and Earth	24
2	Flourishing: Between Humanity and Divinity	46
3	Daring: Between Control and Risk	65
4	Shining: Between Revelation and Hiddenness	79
5	Venturing: Between Certainty and Displacement	99
6	Discovering: Between Prayer and Perception	114
7	Journeying: Between Local and Cosmic	125
8	Trusting: Between Memory and Hope	147
9	Engaging: Between Transfiguration and Disfiguration	160
10	Dancing: Between Mystical and Prophetic	178
Bibliography		195

Images and Credits

1	Mount Tabor, village of Daburiyya in foreground, Wikipedia Commons	23
2	Icon of the Transfiguration by Theophan the Greek, 1408	45
3	Struggle for control: Arch of Crusader Fortress atop Tabor, Author	64
4	Mount Hermon from Lebanon, mylebanonguide.com	78
5	Cloud over Tabor, Author	98
6	Icon of the Transfiguration by Andrei Rublev, 1404	113
7	Light above Tabor Basilica, Author	124
8	Basilica of the Transfiguration, Duns Scotus Bible Centre www2.dsbiblecentre.org	146
9	Hiroshima Bomb, Feast of the Transfiguration 1945, www.historyonthenet.com	159
10	Transfiguration by Raphael, 1520	177

Introduction

EXPLOSIVE, ESOTERIC, ENIGMATIC—THESE ARE ways that the event of the Transfiguration has been viewed. It's been called surreal, an irrelevance. But as a mystery pulsating at the very heart of the Gospel—a watershed in Mark, at its very center, the pivotal turning point in Jesus' ministry—it in fact reveals crucial aspects of Christian living. Looking through the lens of life-giving paradox, this book uncovers its secrets and unleashes its significance for discipleship in troubled times. This hermeneutical key unlocks unexpected insights and allows the light of the Transfiguration to shine into crucial contemporary concerns and crises, as we discover the energy and dynamic of paradox. Drawing on the wisdom and experience of a wide variety of sources—from patristic teachers, spiritual writers, orthodox liturgies, present-day scholarship, as well as from the author's years researching and teaching in the Holy Land—this resource becomes a kaleidoscope of the Transfiguration, widening perspectives and, with a certain edginess, confronts us with transformative challenges. This is not a devotional book, though it will increase a sense of awe and enchantment. It is not a commentary on texts, though it will attend to the Greek gospels. It is a springboard for reinvigorated Christian discipleship, uniquely approaching the Transfiguration through the prism and magnifying glass of paradox—inviting us not to solve a puzzle but to live a mystery, ever more deeply, ever more creatively.

    This is a resource for individuals or groups. It can be used by spiritual directors or spiritual teachers as a retreat, whether personal or corporate; by preachers and theological students. Questions for reflection and prayer exercises in each chapter make it ideal for study groups. Most of all, it is offered as a stimulus to discipleship for all. We will see in this book how the Transfiguration relates to:

- ecology and our care of the earth
- sexuality and identity
- healing and wellness
- lifestyle and re-ordering priorities
- engaging with injustice
- living with change
- welcoming the displaced
- everyday mysticism
- responding courageously and imaginatively to the needs of our world

Handling Paradox

It is a bit like handing an explosive—it could go off at any moment! It is a catalyst triggering a reaction. That is the point: paradox is not there to comfort us or confirm us in our thinking, but to disturb and stimulate. Consider the different ways in which two seemingly-opposite elements can enter into a relationship—this is the dynamic of paradox. When very different ideas come face-to-face, something happens. We move beyond co-existence or juxtaposition towards a new, life-giving relationship generating:

- interaction, intersection or meeting
- cross-fertilization and inter-penetration
- mutual questioning and dialectic conversations
- subversion of duality thinking, reframing binary mindset
- connections across an abyss
- creative tensions and reciprocity between opposites
- frisson of insights and birthing of fresh ideas

It is akin to meeting the Other: the two elements begin an encounter to be marked by mutual respect, listening to one another, discovering the charism or gifting in the Other. And one becomes changed, maybe, in the light of the Other. As Gadamer writes of tradition meeting the present day: "something comes into being that had not existed before and that exists from now on. . . something emerges that is contained in neither of the partners by themselves."[1] Paradox can be unpredictable but creative!

A Divided World

The world oscillates endlessly between hope and suffering. There also seems to be a natural human tendency towards polarization, keeping things apart. It has to do with being in control, trying to make sense of things neatly, seeing things in black and white, but as we know it can lead to fundamentalism, racism, homophobia, fear of the other. We feel safer when we oppose, judge, differentiate, label and compare. Today, we live in a polarized word: republican vs. democrat, conservative vs. labor, protestant vs. catholic, east vs. west, science vs. religion. Everyday we see the divides of rich vs. poor, the haves and the have-nots. The Holy Land itself faces the greatest tragedy of Palestinian pitted against Israeli, Arab against Jew. "Divide and rule" has long been a maxim of war, leading of course to different versions of apartheid and segregation.

Bifurcation is today's default position. It has been said, we live in a "tit for tat universe."[2] Computers, which increasingly rule our lives, are based on a binary system. McAfee Brown calls this addiction to duality "the great fallacy."[3] Hughes writes of our tendency to maintain a "split spirituality."[4]

CONTRADICTIONS IN CHRISTIAN FAITH

Paradox opens up a different way—that of "both/and" instead of "either/or"—and pulses as a vital dynamic in Christian faith and practice. What divides do we experience?

There is the constant tension between ideal and reality. We are told about our capacity to bear the divine Spirit—that we are made in the image and likeness of God—but we are all too aware of our mortality, limitations, fragility and failure. With St Paul we cry out: "I do not understand my own

---

1. Gadamer, *Truth and Method*, 462.
2. Rohr, *Naked Now*, 77.
3. McAfee Brown, *Spirituality and Liberation*.
4. Hughes, *God in All Things*, ch.1.

actions. For I do not do what I want, but I do the very thing I hate... Who will rescue me.?" (Rom 7:15,24). We are, in Luther's words, *simul justus et peccator*: justified yet sinful.

There are other oppositions we wrestle with. We know we must strive to help build Christian community, but are summoned at times to solitude. I must come to terms with the child and adult in me, masculine and feminine sides to my unique personality. Theologians argue about the interplay between nature and grace, others about determinism and freedom, nature vs. nurture. God is at once immanent and transcendent, close at hand yet seemingly faraway. How can we make sense of these contradictions?

Sadly, Christian spirituality became infected with divisive, dualistic thinking since early centuries embraced Platonic thought. This gave rise to disastrous polarities in Christian thinking, as things were pitched against one another. Heaven was opposed to earth, the body to the spirit, spirituality divorced from sexuality. Politics and prayer were to be kept separate. Sacred and secular were delineated with barriers, as if they were two separate realms, holy and profane, church and world set against each other. Throughout the history of Christian spirituality, heavenly-minded contemplative life has been exalted above the active apostolate in the world. Thomas Aquinas in his *Summa Theologica* (question 182) gives eight reasons why the angelic life of prayer is a higher calling and attracts more merit than the active life of service. Counsels of perfection encouraged an elitist view of spirituality, for those who were able to make withdrawal from the world.

Paradox in Spirituality and Faith

But paradox has a creative role too in the exploration of Christian faith. The apostles were described as those who "have turned the world upside down" (Acts 17:6). Paul affirms the paradox: "For you know the generous act of our Lord Jesus Christ, that though he was rich, yet for your sakes he became poor, so that you through his poverty might become rich" (2 Cor 8:9). He sees the Christian vocation in highly paradoxical terms:

> We are treated as imposters, and yet are true;
> as unknown, and yet are well known;
> as dying, and see—we are alive;
> as punished, and yet not killed; as sorrowful, yet always rejoicing;
> as poor, yet making many rich;
> as having nothing, yet possessing everything. (2 Cor 6:8–10)

INTRODUCTION

Paul realizes the importance of paradox:

> For God's foolishness is wiser than human wisdom,
> God's weakness is stronger than human strength...
> God chose what is foolish in the world to shame the wise;
> God chose what is weak in the world to shame the strong;
> God chose what is low and despised in the world, things that are not,
> to reduce to nothing things that are. (1 Cor 1:25,27–28)
> For the wisdom of this world is foolishness with God. (1 Cor 3:19)

Paradox lies at the heart of Christian belief. Hymnody communicates something of the astonishment and wonder at this:

> O wonder of wonders, which none can unfold:
> The Ancient of Days is an hour or two old;
> the Maker of all things is made of the earth,
> man is worshipped by angels, and God comes to birth.[5]

The Nicene Creed declares that "Light from Light" was "crucified under Pontius Pilate." The Incarnation and the Cross, the very center of Christian faith, consist of paradox. The Good Friday hymns of the Orthodox Church exult:

> Today He who hung the earth upon the waters is hung upon the Cross.
> He who is King of the angels is arrayed in a crown of thorns.
> He who in Jordan set Adam free receives blows upon His face.
> The Bridegroom of the Church is transfixed with nails.
> The Son of the Virgin is pierced with a spear.
> We venerate Thy Passion, O Christ.
> Show us also Thy glorious Resurrection.[6]

In spirituality, dualistic thinking has created unnecessary distances and opened up uncalled-for chasms. Where God is thought of as something "out there" or "up there" the Divine is seen as remote and unapproachable. But Christian spirituality celebrates the God within, and the breakthrough to non-dualistic thinking comes precisely when the prayer of contemplation—mystic prayer—begins to shorten the distance between humans and God. John Macquarrie entitles his introduction to Christian mysticism *Two*

---

5. Hymn "The Great God of Heaven" by H.R. Bramley (1833–1917). See also Nativity hymns of the Orthodox Church in Mother Mary and Ware (trans.), *Festal Menaion*. For a modern example, see Graham Kendrick's *Meekness and Majesty*.

6. Fifteenth Antiphon of Good Friday Matins in Mother Mary and Ware, *Lenten Triodion*, 565ff.

Worlds Are Ours.[7] As we shall see, prayer becomes the entry into a different way of knowing, an alternative way of perceiving reality. Prayer might begin with a sense of God beyond: "Our Father who art in heaven." But it dares to pray "thy Kingdom come" and moves to an awareness of the God within: "Thy will be done on earth as it is in heaven." Jesus leads us from a dualistic view of things to a unitive understanding. He leads us to reconciliation.

JESUS—LIVING IN A POLARIZED WORLD

Jesus lived in a bitterly divided and polarized world. In the first century society was falling apart and riven by conflict and opposing forces. Jew was pitted against Gentile, as the Jewish people tried to maintain ritual purity and sense of identity in a land contaminated by military occupation. Zealots warred against Roman might. Pharisees and Sadducees were at each other's necks. The scribes and the lawyers were at loggerheads. The Essenes opposed and defied the Temple authorities. It was a fragmenting society, riven with divisions and splits in the population.

Studies in cultural anthropology and historical sociology illumine the dynamics and mindsets prevailing in first century society, especially the status/ shame divide.[8] In the society of Jesus' time, people were kept apart by a sense of hierarchy, in which honor was fawned upon patriarchal families and the well-to-do, while at the opposite end of the spectrum, shame was spat at social nobodies: not only obvious social outcasts like tax collectors (deemed to be collaborators with the Romans) and prostitutes, but also children and women. It was a painfully polarized society in which the sick and maimed were excluded from the Temple and where those who did not "fit" were mercilessly marginalized.

But this human tendency to divide and rule, to split things up so they can be controlled and manipulated, infected not only culture and social structures, but the very structure of religious thinking itself. Even within the Hebrew Scriptures one detects dualistic thinking at times:

- Heaven is remote and God's ways distant (Isa 55:8,9).
- Enemies are to be slaughtered (Ps 139:19–22).

---

7. Macquarrie, *Two Worlds.*
8. Malina, *New Testament World;* Meier, *Marginal Jew.*

Such tribalism stands in opposition with universalism: "Turn to me and be saved, all the ends of the earth!" (Isa 45:22).

The Gospels give evidence of dualistic thinking persisting among ordinary people:

- Sinners are to be stoned not welcomed (John 8:1–11).
- The outside of the cup is more important than the inside (Matt 23:25).
- Outer compliance seems more respectable than the inner heart (Matt 23:17,18).
- Tithing and religious observance are divorced from issues of justice and mercy (Matt 23:23).
- The chosen people are superior to gentiles (Mark 7:27).

A UNIFYING VISION

According to Luke, Jesus begins his ministry in Nazareth with the announcement that he is coming to bring together things that are separated. He quotes from Isaiah 61:

> "The Spirit of the Lord is upon me,
>   because he has anointed me
>   to bring good news to the poor.
> He has sent me to proclaim release to the captives
>   and recovery of sight to the blind,
>   to let the oppressed go free,
> to proclaim the year of the Lord's favor." (Luke 4:18,19)

Did Jesus gain this heart-felt desire from his reading of the prophet Isaiah? Jesus was much inspired by the prophet, and there are clues in the gospels that he saw in Isaiah's "servant songs" (for example, Isa 53) a sketch of his unfolding vocation. The prophet reveals a longing for unity and for elements that are often divorced or separated to be united:

> The wolf shall live with the lamb,
> the leopard shall lie down with the kid . . .
> The cow and the bear shall graze (Isa 11:6,7)

Maybe Jesus was inspired by the psalms' non-dualistic call to worship:

> Wild animals and all cattle, creeping things and flying birds! . . .
> Young men and women alike, old and young together!
> (Ps 148:10,12)

The Gospels are full of episodes in which Jesus crosses boundaries and breaks down barriers. The presence of women is welcomed by Jesus (Luke 8:3; 23:49) and Mary Magdalene becomes first witness of the resurrection. In Jerusalem, throwing down the tables of the money-changers in the Temple, he welcomes outcasts and the ritually unclean: "The blind and the lame came to him in the temple, and he cured them" (Matt 21:14).

Notice how many of Jesus sayings are about overcoming separation, loss and division. He sees the potential for things once separated coming together:

- The woman is reunited with her lost coin.
- The shepherd once again embraces his sheep.
- The yeast is mixed with the flour.
- The vine is joined to the branches.
- The birds come to roost in the branches.
- Things old and new are to be treasured.
- The enemy is to be loved.
- The prodigal is restored to his father.
- The wounded Jewish traveler rests in the arms of a hated Samaritan.

It is precisely in a context of prevailing dualistic mindsets that Jesus develops his radical unifying and inclusive vision of the Kingdom of God. With all his heart he longs to bring all people together as one in their dignity as beloved and cherished children of God. In the holy city Jesus will cry out his heart's longing: "Jerusalem, Jerusalem . . . How often have I desired to gather your children together as a hen gathers her brood under her wings, and you were not willing!" (Luke 13:34). Jesus' desire is for the unity of the world: "Then people will come from east and west, from north and south, and will eat in the kingdom of God" (Luke 13:29).

The kingdom of God is a topsy-turvy kingdom. It is both "now" and "not yet". Things are inside out, round the wrong way, at least to conventional thinking: this is a subversive wisdom that undermines usual patterns of thought.

Somehow he is both Son of God and Son of Mary. Crazily, he turns out to be both human and divine. The immaterial Word became flesh. The Incarnation smashes into pieces the divides between flesh and spirit. Now all is one in Christ. As in the Orthodox icon of the resurrection, where the

INTRODUCTION

Risen Jesus extends one hand to Eve and one to Adam and pulls them out of their tombs to new life, Jesus unites the paradoxes: "in him all things hold together" (Col 1:17). At his baptism heaven is torn open: heaven and earth themselves are brought into a new relation. The *Gloria* puts it: "Heaven and earth are full of your glory!" Jesus is the lion and the lamb, victim and victor, wounded healer, servant leader, the King who reigns from the Cross, alpha and omega. He models a unity of action and contemplation, busyness and stillness. His sojourn in the Decapolis where he makes the deaf hear and the dumb speak (Mark 7:37) shows us that contradictions can turn to paradoxes, and wholeness comes from uniting opposing elements.

"Let Us Go Over to the Other Side"

What is striking in the Gospels is how Jesus moves to and fro, across and back across the Sea of Galilee. Have you ever noticed how many times in the gospels Jesus says: "Let us go over to the *other* side"? He asks his disciples to leave the security of Capernaum, a conservative, traditional, mainly Jewish town, and to traverse the waters to go to enemy territory, pagan, heathen Gentile terrain, Greco-Roman land, shores where unclean demoniacs and Gadarene pigs lurk uncontrolled. He wanted to lead them to areas on the very frontier of the Roman Empire: the group of ten cities marked by Greek culture, nine of which lay beyond the confines of ancient Israel (located in present day Jordan and Syria). Normally, it is a place to be avoided: to go there would contaminate the devout Jew. But Jesus calls his disciples to quit their safety zone and risk encounter with the Other, with those who are definitely "not us." (Even today, the Golan Heights are a no-go military zone.) But today, as then, it is as if the two opposite sides of the Lake, facing each other across the dangerous waters, want to be in dialogue with each other, each posing its questions to the other. It is as if they want to talk. The two sides actually need each other!

He repeatedly criss-crosses the stormy waters. He wishes to touch and embrace both Jew and Gentile, both the ritually clean and the unclean. He moves between two domains, between two world views, and is at home in either. Again, it is not a case of "either/or" but of "both/and". Jesus is the "go-between God."[9] Jesus truly is a mediator, one who moves between parties at variance.

9. The title of John V. Taylor's classic work on the Holy Spirit

JESUS TEACHES BY PARADOX

Paradoxical Blessings

The Beatitudes bring together a selection of jaw-dropping, astonishing paradoxes:

> When Jesus saw the crowds, he went up the hillside, and sat down. His disciples came to him. He took a deep breath, and began his teaching:
>
> *Blessings on the poor in spirit!*
>   The kingdom of heaven is yours.
> *Blessings on the mourners!*
>   You're going to be comforted.
> *Blessings on the meek!*
>   You're going to inherit the earth.
> *Blessings on people who hunger and thirst for God's justice!*
>   You're going to be satisfied.
> *Blessings on the merciful!*
>   You'll receive mercy yourselves.
> *Blessings on the pure in heart!*
>   You will see God.
> *Blessings on the peacemakers!*
>   You'll be called God's children.
> *Blessings on people persecuted for the sake of justice!*
>   The kingdom of heaven is already yours! (NTFE)

Paradoxical Words

In his teaching, Jesus transforms divisive contradictions that erode life into paradoxes that give life:

- "Those who want to save their lives will lose them, and those who lose their lives will save them."
- "The first will be last and the last first."
- "He makes his sun to rise on rich and poor alike, righteous and unrighteous."
- "Whoever desires to become great among you shall be your servant; and whoever desires to be first among you shall be the bondslave of all."

INTRODUCTION

- "Whoever exalts oneself will be humbled: whoever humbles oneself will be exalted."
- Superficially noble admirable structures (and lives) turn out to be the opposite: "Woe to you, scribes and Pharisees, hypocrites! For you are like whitewashed tombs, which on the outside look beautiful, but inside they are full of the bones of the dead and of all kinds of filth. So you also on the outside look righteous to others, but inside you are full of hypocrisy and lawlessness" (Matt 23:27,28). Those who put themselves forward as guides turn out to be blind (Matt 15:14).
- It's not what goes into a person that makes them bad, but what comes out of their heart (Matt 15:20).
- "You are not to be called rabbi, for you have one teacher, and you are all students. And call no one your father on earth, for you have one Father—the one in heaven" (Matt 23:8–10).

Paradox in Parables

There is a correlation between Jesus' choice of parable as his major teaching method and his frequent use of paradox. Parable essentially means "a comparison"—literally "throwing something beside something else", hence "a juxtaposition," from *para* "alongside" and *bolē* "a throwing, casting". As a translation of the Hebrew word *mashal*, the word parable can also refer to a riddle.

Meanwhile, the ancient Greeks were well aware that a paradox can take us outside our usual way of thinking. They combined the prefix *para* ("beyond" or "outside of") with the verb *dokein* ("to think"), forming *paradoxos*, an adjective meaning "contrary to expectation." The Greek *paradoxon* means "incredible statement or opinion," opposite to conventional.

Jesus combines parable and paradox. A paradox is a statement that appears at first to be contradictory, but upon reflection then makes sense in a quite unexpected way. Paradox is not a compromise, a meeting halfway. Rather it becomes a vortex generating a creative interplay of ideas, a dialogue that actually listens to both sides. It is a matrix and environment for thinking "outside the box" and discarding unfruitful inherited notions or conventions past their "sell-by" date. It may be an uncomfortable place—unsettling, but within its tensions new insights flare up. It is an heuristic teaching method to allow students to find answers without being instructed.

Jesus does not teach by delivering lectures. The synoptic gospels rarely contain discourses. He teaches by way of parable, metaphor and story that trigger the imagination and stimulate the soul, not by precepts and propositions educating only the mind. As in the parables, he does not instruct so much as evoke and provoke. He seeks a response, engaging heart and mind. Is Jesus the answer—or the question? Jesus does not pronounce dogmas to be assented to, he presents puzzles to be enjoyed! Jesus does not give definitions but invitations, and leads us towards wonder and wisdom, towards formation, not information. Paradoxes do not close down the subject with an air of gravity and finality. They open up new horizons, fresh ways of thinking.

Here we are reaching the very heart of Jesus' approach. We are not being cajoled into submission by doctrines that require our obedience but are being invited to explore the truth that will set us free. We are not being called to assent to concepts but to conception and new birth.

We are being loved into the Kingdom, teased into it by a Lover—not admitted to a kingdom upon completion of an entrance exam. We are not harangued but wooed into the Kingdom. By his paradoxical words Jesus awakens the soul, inspires, disturbs—not instructs. He summons us to sound the depths. His words are like seeds impregnating the soul and secretly, inwardly gestating and bearing fruit. They nourish and nurture not nag.

JESUS ACTS BY PARADOX

Paradoxical Actions

In addition Jesus embodies and communicates his message through crazy actions:

- He picks wheat on the Sabbath day.
- He calls a child into the midst of the disciples to teach them about true greatness.
- In the midst of the storm on the lake, he falls asleep, his head on a cushion.

- He embraces the untouchable leper.
- He allows dubious women to anoint him, and dry him with their flowing hair.
- He positions himself next to a questionable woman at the well.
- He does enigmatic things, drawing in the dust.
- He walks on water and invites Peter to join him.
- He makes his solemn entry into Jerusalem seated on an ass!

JESUS REVEALS BY PARADOX

The Paradox of the Kingdom of God

In Mark's perspective, Jesus at the outset announces his intention to revolutionize and radically shake up people's thinking: "The time is fulfilled, and the Kingdom of God has come near; repent and believe in the good news" (1:15). So, the opening lines of Jesus' proclamation entail a call to "repent." We usually read this in a moralistic way, calling us to penitence, but as recent writers have reminded us, this is in fact a summons to an utterly different way of seeing reality.[10] The word is literally *meta*, meaning "beyond" or "large", and *noia*, which translates as "mind." Jesus is calling us to "go beyond the mind" or "go into the big mind." He is inviting us to a fresh way of seeing things, a new consciousness. He is demanding that we let go of our former defensive dualistic paradigms and make the transition into a new vision of things that is summed up in the metaphor of the "Kingdom of God."

Jesus proclaims his central theme and dream—the Kingdom of God—through paradoxes within parables. We see this in a focused way in Matthew 13 which shares with us "the secrets of the Kingdom of Heaven." In six ways Jesus says that the Kingdom of God is like

- Wheat and weeds allowed to grow together.
- The microscopic mustard seed becomes greatest shrub.
- A tiny amount of yeast leavens a big loaf.
- A whole field concealing buried treasure is worth everything.

10. See Rohr, *Naked Now*.

- The purchase of one fine pearl is worth a person's entire savings to acquire.
- Wise ones bring out things both new and old from the treasure house.

THE POWER OF PARADOX TO EXPLORE TRANSFIGURATION

If Jesus, then, uses paradox as a key teaching method, and if he uses prophetic actions to embody and encapsulate and communicate his message, may we not approach the Transfiguration in this way? A. D. A. Moses observes, "In the West, contemporary scholarship has not given the transfiguration story as significant a place in the discussion on New Testament theology as might be expected."[11] Biblical scholar Terence L. Donaldson pinpoints one of the challenges:

> The task of discovering a single interpretative key that will allow the Transfiguration's many associations and links to be seen as parts of an overall pattern has proven to be virtually impossible.[12]

Might it be that we have stumbled on such a missing key?

> He said to them, "Truly I tell you, there are some standing here who will not taste death until they see that the kingdom of God has come with power." Six days later, Jesus took with him Peter and James and John, and led them up a high mountain apart, by themselves. And he was transfigured before them (Mark 9:1,2)

Might it be that, at this pivotal watershed moment in his ministry, Jesus chooses transfiguration to reveal the Kingdom of God—precisely through the power of its paradoxes? Tabor turns out to be the precipice of great discoveries.

My Experience

I myself have danced between the paradoxes. The son and grandson of a Presbyterian minister, I grew up in the Methodist Church, becoming an Anglican in the catholic tradition at the age of 21, rejoicing in the

---

11. Moses, *Matthew's Transfiguration Story*, 13.
12. Donaldson, *Jesus on the Mountain*, 136.

INTRODUCTION

transcendence of Anglo-Catholic worship while cherishing John and Charles Wesley. After my BD at King's College London, I lived for a year in the Armenian Orthodox Seminary in Jerusalem (under the Philip Usher Scholarship), learning classical Armenian at the Hebrew University and singing in the Armenian choir of the Holy Sepulcher. Upon Ordination I studied spirituality for a year at Catholic Heythrop College in London, completing a MA in spirituality via the Wesleyan Nazarene College, Manchester. My doctoral researches into ministerial formation took me to places of ministerial education as diverse as Oak Hill Bible College and seminaries in Syria, Armenia, and Ethiopia.

I find myself belonging to a church infamous for its paradoxes, somehow embracing catholic and protestant, high and low, the innovative and the traditional. As director of continuing ministerial education, in a large Anglican diocese, charged with designing training programs for newly-ordained curates, the challenge was bringing black-suited Anglo-Catholics into relationship with T-shirt clad evangelicals. They had studied for the ordained ministry quite separately in their respective seminaries or bible colleges, with few occasions to encounter other traditions. But where individuals find themselves equal within a learning community, breakthroughs are possible. They were not there as delegates of a tradition—they were there as fellow learners. And we found that the secret was discovering the lost art of listening to one another. We might even glimpse something new, or something of ancient wisdom!

In Jerusalem as course director of an Anglican college the challenge was to build a learning community from a diversity of cultures representing diverse theological world-views. Nigerian literalists found themselves alongside American liberals. But both were on a journey. Both were finding out what it means to be a pilgrim—requiring that self-protective walls crumble and prejudices melt in the middle eastern sun. When diverse or even opposing groups found that they were being called to become not only a learning community but also a pilgrim band on the move through the Holy Land, hearts and minds were opened as they discovered on the journey contemplative and reflective spaces.

As a Franciscan, I am committed to the Principles of the Third Order, Society of St Francis: "The Order sets out, in the name of Christ, to break down barriers between people and to seek equality for all. We aim to spread a spirit of love and reconciliation among all people. . .Our chief object is to reflect that openness to all which was characteristic of Jesus." Until recently, as the Spirituality Adviser to the Diocese of Cyprus and the Gulf, it was a privilege to engage with many different cultures. These days on Sundays I might be taking a service for the Anglo-Catholics or the Moravians!

Reflecting on the Transfiguration in many visits to Mount Tabor and in a retreat on the summit, I offer this resource in a world where we crave for wholeness and healing among the divided.

INTO LIMINAL SPACE

In this book the concept of liminality lies in the background, as a portal for understanding paradoxes. The concept of liminality is inspiring, unsettling and energizing. In entering liminal space, you leave behind your former ideals and conventions, the status quo, the ordinary routines, inherited mind-sets. You also leave behind your safety zone, you quit your place of security. You step out into a space where you will see things differently, where your world-view might be shattered, where your existing priorities might be turned upside down. You cross a border and go beyond your usual limits. What had been a barrier now becomes a threshold, a stepping stone into a larger spiritual adventure. The liminal spaces into which Jesus leads us are places of radical unmaking and unlearning—uncomfortable spaces where we're called to be utterly vulnerable to God, and from which we will re-enter the world quite changed, even converted! The *limen* is the threshold, the place of departure, a springboard into a fresh way of doing things. . .

The concept of liminality derives from Arnold van Gennep's 1909 study *Rites de Passage*, an anthropological study of ritual in communities.[13] Victor Turner took this further in his studies among tribes in Zambia.[14] He noticed that the transitional phase was a testing process of undoing and remaking. The place of liminality thus becomes a place of ambiguity and confusion as one world is left behind, one thought-world, and things are shaken up before one can re-enter society with a different perspective, indeed a different social status. This is the place of "anti-structure": the opposite to the world of normality and of usual structures and roles, the place of status quo, "business as usual." But while it is a place of uncertainty, it is precisely here that the person clarifies his or her sense of identity and

---

13. Van Gennep, *Rites of Passage*.

14. Turner, *Ritual Process*. He explores pilgrimage as a liminal experience in Turner, *Image and Pilgrimage*.

purpose. Things are discovered in the liminal zone that can't be found in the routines of normal life.

We find ourselves in a space where we may long with nostalgia for old, familiar certainties and securities, for the traditional and safe. But we find, instead, that it is *precisely* here, in such risky places as Tabor, that Christ waits to meet us, to reveal himself to us. The prayer-event of the transfiguration resonates very clearly with van Gennep's three stages of liminality which cast light on the journey of prayer that each of us can make.

Three Movements

1 Ascent

First, there is *separation*, involving a metaphorical death or breaking with past practices and expectations. The three disciples separate themselves from the rest of the disciples and they create a distance from the demands of ministry and from the pressing crowds. But they do this as a response to an invitation from Christ—indeed, it is he who is doing the separating: "Six days later Jesus *took* with him Peter and James and John, and *led them* up a high mountain, *by themselves*" (Mark 9:2). Jesus is drawing them away from the hectic world of Caesarea Philippi and into another world. He is taking them to the wind-blown mountain top to encounter the untamable God. He is leading them into solitude.

This resonates with our own journey of prayer. Prayer begins with a response to Christ's invitation to go higher. It begins with a decision to accompany Jesus into the upper reaches of prayer. The ascent of the mountain will take stamina, resolution and determination. They will be plenty of distractions and the temptation to take shortcuts. What is needed is singleness of heart to go with Jesus, wherever he leads.

Many spiritual writers have explored prayer as an ascent to God, especially male authors.[15] John Climacus (579–649), the abbot of the monastery of St Catherine's, at the foot of Mount Sinai itself, suggested in his work *The Ladder of Divine Ascent* that there were thirty rungs on the staircase to heaven, thirty virtues to be nurtured. Bonaventure (1217–74) in *The Journey of the Mind into God* writes of the "mind's ascent to God." In the English

---

15. Borysenko, *A Woman's Journey to God*, contrasts male spirituality, as in the ascent model of Jacob's ladder, in successive linear stages, with female spirituality symbolized in Sarah's circle, a more relational, immanent model: less climbing, more nurturing!

tradition, Walter Hilton (d.1396) described prayer in terms of ascending a *Ladder of Perfection*. In the sixteenth century, John of the Cross centers his masterpiece *The Ascent of Mount Carmel* on the model of going up to God in prayer. A recurring theme is the necessity for detachment—withdrawal from daily demands in order to enter prayer, conceived as a sacred space, as a different world.[16] In the fourth century, Basil the Great had written: "Now this withdrawal [*anachoresis*, retreat] does not mean that we should leave the world bodily, but rather break loose from the ties of "sympathy" of the soul with the body."[17] Basil extols the virtues of making a retreat from activity, for a few minutes, or hours, or days. He says that, for a season, we have to cut our ties, loosen our grip and grasp on activities, let go of our attachments and of our worries. This is so we can become wholly available to God in prayer.

2 Transformation

In von Gennep and Turner's understanding, the initiate enters into a place of transformation: this is the *liminal state* where those to be initiated, for example young people into adulthood, must face challenges to their sense of identity and a process of re-formation. "As he was praying, the appearance of his face *changed* . . ." The Eastern Church, celebrating the event as the Feast of the *Metamorphosis*, considers that it is the disciples, not Christ, who are changed, as we shall see: perception is enlarged, understanding transfigured. The change occurs in the disciples to the extent that they allow themselves to become not spectators but participants in the divinity revealed to them. The Transfiguration event is truly a *limen*, a threshold of the Divine as the disciples are caught up into the radiant light of Christ.

3 Return

Von Gennep's third phase of liminality is *aggregation* or reintegration into the community as a changed person with a sharpened sense of values. Jesus and the disciples descend the mountain, to re-engage with the demands of ministry and to begin the walk towards the way of the Cross. For Mark, the event of the Transfiguration is a pivotal moment in the course of his gospel,

---

16. For a critique of the ascent model see Miles, *Image and Practice of Holiness*.
17. "Letter 2" in Barrois, *The Fathers Speak*.

INTRODUCTION

and leads to the journey to Calvary. The experience of mystical or receptive prayer may be for us, too, the catapult into dangerous and demanding situations where we will find ourselves fulfilling Jesus' injunction to "take up the Cross and follow me"—words which preface the Transfiguration (Mark 8:34). The event is bracketed by predictions of passion. The experience of "supernatural prayer" (to use Teresa's phrase), as Moses and Elijah found out for themselves, may mark a transition into the next phase of costly obedience to God. The foaming demoniac, desperate for healing, awaits the disciples at the foot of the mountain.

OUTLINE OF THIS BOOK

In chapter 1, as we make our ascent of the mount of Transfiguration, we find ourselves caught between heaven and earth. As we reflect on our call to live as citizens of heaven, we review our commitments to our ailing planet. We are inspired by Orthodox liturgical texts and by the stunning iconography of Andrei Rublev (1360–1430) and Theophan the Greek (1340–1410). To live the transfigured life between earth and heaven, we rediscover the paradox that the Kingdom of Heaven is beneath our feet.

In chapter 2 we face the paradox of our humanity: an astonishing capacity for the Divine amidst our frailty and brokenness. We allow ourselves to be dumbfounded at the possibility that we might be called to experience deification, even in this life, as Gregory Palamas and Maximos teach us. And the intriguingly-named lay community on Mount Tabor, *MONDO X*—meaning "unknown world"—gives us an inspirational example of such transformation. We realize that to live a transfigured life is to be aware of our mortality—and thus be gentle with ourselves—and at the same time to rejoice in our God-given dignity, to celebrate our true identity in Christ and to flourish in our divine potentiality.

Thirdly, with Peter we next encounter both the light and the cloud of Tabor. We wonder how we might permit ourselves to pray in quite different ways—walking the *via positiva* and the *via negativa*. With the help of Gregory of Nyssa and Dionysius, we see how the Christian life is strung between control and risk, between knowing God and experiencing God's unknowability. In this chapter we see how living the transfigured life is paradoxical indeed—to find life, we must lose it—we must release our grip on the tiller, in order to guided divinely forward. We give up control, but we find everything. Vulnerability is not a condition to be avoided—it turns out to be the precondition of discovering God!

Chapter 4 introduces us to a further paradoxical theme emerging from the Transfiguration: how this revealing event is strangely to be kept secret, for the time being. We find our own lives of prayer are held within the tension and double call to both hiddenness and proclamation. We learn how the Franciscan Third Order (TSSF) had to work this out in the last century. We explore how living a transfigured life entails a daily paradox of involvement and detachment, availability and needful reticence. Like Jesus on Tabor, we live lives that reveal and proclaim openly the love of God, while safeguarding the inner spaces of prayer, reflection and contemplation.

In chapter 5 we see in the figures of Moses and Elijah both immovable representatives of the Tradition—pillars of the establishment—and pilgrims exemplifying adventure and risk-taking. They invite us to reflect on our lives as lived between the polarities of certainty and odyssey. We also recognize how Moses and Elijah represent displaced people, and ask what place they might have in our prayer, assisted by Gregory of Nyssa and Dorothy Soelle. We ponder how living a transfigured life requires us to remain rooted and grounded and firm in our faith while, at the same time, being ready to embrace change and challenge. The transfigured life invites us too to crave a reckless generosity of heart towards the Other.

In chapter 6 we revisit the Orthodox insight that the *metamorphosis* atop Tabor was not only the change wrought in Jesus' appearance, but the shifts experienced by the disciples, in particular a transformation in the way they see things. Their eyes are opened to new realities—as Lossky and Palamas show us, their perception is fundamentally altered. Recent commentators—Macquarrie, Moltmann and Rowan Williams—help us understand how our own perceptions can change in the course of praying. We see how a transfigured life requires that we give up on narrow, prescriptive, hectoring types of prayer. It invites us to be poised and ready, in times of prayer, to be changed—to be aware that we might be standing on the brink of new discoveries of the Gospel. It invites us to be set to shift perceptions of the Divine.

Chapter 7 leads us to reflect on the interplay between the local and the universal. We ponder the paradox in the Transfiguration between an event in a particular, limited locale and its cosmic significance. Teilhard de Chardin helps us catch a mind-expanding vision of the Cosmic Christ. We wonder, too, how we can live in solidarity with suffering people in different

INTRODUCTION

parts of the globe, while remaining attentive and responsive to the part of the planet where we actually live.

In chapter 8 we experience the pull between the past and the future. We sense too the tension between the "now" and "not yet" of the Kingdom. We see how the historical event of the Transfiguration points forward to the Resurrection, Parousia and Eschaton. We learn how we can live between the poles of remembrance and hope—indeed, between time and eternity. De Caussade introduces us to the transformative idea of "the sacrament of the present moment". We discover in this chapter how living a transfigured life is to have a sense of salvation history and of how God's purposes have unfolded in the past, while clinging to a confidence that "God is working his purpose out". The Transfiguration equips us to live in hope, ever ready, at each moment of the day, to welcome the transforming light of Christ into our very midst!

Chapter 9 confronts us with the reality that the landscape in which Mount Tabor rises is bloodied by violence and warfare through the millennia, from ancient times to the present. Mark Twain called Tabor's setting "the battleground of the nations." We see how the Transfiguration points us inexorably, inescapably, towards the plain of human suffering—and invites us to find in such situations unexpected signs of grace. The Kingdom of God is encountered in glory and pain, and we will learn about the Orthodox experience of "joyful sorrow." To live a transfigured life, we must be ready to face suffering—but not in a spirit of resignation or fatalism. On the contrary, we greet it as a potential arena of grace and commit ourselves to see how, into situations of pain, fragments of God's reign might break through.

In chapter 10 we wrestle with the central paradox expressed by the hymn: "It's good Lord to be here/ but we may not remain." The two religious traditions atop Tabor, Benedictine and Franciscan, help us ask how contemplation can be balanced by action, stillness by movement. But the example of Jesus takes us beyond this dichotomy of competing calls—he shows us how we can live as a contemplative *in* action, guarding a heart of listening and prayer in the very midst of the maelstrom of ministry. We see how a transfigured life invites us to dance in the interplay between the mystical and the prophetic. As we ready ourselves to turn to the world, we seek in all our activities to foster an inward stillness, an attentiveness to God at the center of demands.

Paradox: Not a Panacea but a Promise

Parker J. Palmer observes:

> I have heard the term paradox used as if it were an incantation that could magically remove life's tensions and relieve us of responsibility for them. I have heard people use the word to describe the gap between behavior and belief as if the word itself would excuse and even sanctify the contradiction, allowing us to forget about it. But that is what Bonhoeffer called "cheap grace" and nothing could be further from my understanding.
>
> Our first need is not to release the tension but to *live the contradictions*, fully and painfully aware of the poles between which our lives are stretched. As we do so, we will be plunged into paradox, at whose heart we will find transcendence and new life. Our lives will be changed; our beliefs and actions will become more responsive to God's Spirit. But this will happen only as we become engulfed by contradictions that God alone can resolve.[18]

And in one of the wisest books on the subject Esther de Waal encourages us:

> Living with paradox may well not be easy or comfortable. It is not something for the lazy, the complacent, the fanatical. It does however point us the way to truth and life. For as we learn to live with paradox we have to admit that two realities my be equally true; we may be asked to hold together contrasting forces. The closer we come to saying something worthwhile, the more likely it is that paradox will be the only way to express it.[19]

As Michael Ramsey observed:

> The Transfiguration needs to be restored to its rightful place at the heart of Christian theology. . .It is not simply one event among many in Jesus' ministry. On the contrary, it has a function that goes beyond any single episode in the life of Jesus, holding together things that are too often held apart. . .[20]

---

18. Palmer, *Promise of Paradox*, 8.
19. de Waal, *Living with Contradiction*, 23, 34.
20. Ramsey, *Glory of God*, 144.

Mount Tabor, village of Daburiyya in foreground

1

Reaching
Between Heaven and Earth

How is it possible to maintain an eternal perspective in the midst of human anguish? How can our struggles for justice on the earth be linked to our search for heaven? Can the Transfiguration, far from being unworldly and remote, somehow shine fresh light onto the urgent challenges that confront us in today's damaged world? Can an attentiveness to heaven save us from burnout, as we strive to play our part on this vulnerable planet? Can we live grounded lives with a sense of the unfolding purposes of God, so that we are not earth-bound or mundane in our thinking? Can we maintain an eternal perspective without having "our head in the clouds" and keeping our feet on the ground? We can get so wrapped up in the dramas and crises of the present, that we need to pray for the grace to "pass through things temporal that we lose not our hold on things eternal" (Collect, Trinity 4). But do we need to put the world to one side in order to be attentive to higher things? And, how can we live with a certain detachment to the material things of earth while at the same time care deeply for the fabric of the planet? Michael Ramsey observes:

> It is possible to regard the redemptive act of God in Christ in terms so transcendental that nature and history are not seen in real relation to it, or to identify the divine act with nature and history in such a way that the other-worldly tension of the Gospel is

forgotten. Against these distortions the Transfiguration casts its light in protest.¹

In Hebrew cosmology² the heavens are a distant domain:

> For as the heavens are higher than the earth,
> so are my ways higher than your ways
> and my thoughts than your thoughts. (Isa 55:9)

Heaven seems faraway, the abode of the Divine, prompting us to ask with the psalmist:

> O Lord, our Sovereign,
>   You have set your glory above the heavens.
> When I look at your heavens, the work of your hands,
>   the moon and the stars that you have established;
> what are human beings that you are mindful of them,
>   mortals that you care for them? (Ps 8:1–4)

As we ascend the mountain of Transfiguration with Peter, James and John it looks as if we are leaving behind the world below us and escaping from its demands and traumas. Actually, we are being summoned to glimpse heaven and to bathe in its radiant light atop the mountain, while we reverence earth's materiality and physicality. The challenge we face in this chapter, as we are pulled between the celestial and terrestrial, is to avoid two extremes or polarities:

- Being so heavenly-minded that we are of no earthly use—"super-spiritual"—the essence of Christian life is securing our place in heaven.

or

- Being so tied up in our practical and political commitments to ecology or social action that we loose sight of the Transcendent and our heavenly calling.

This paradox can be represented in church architecture. In the twelfth century Abbot Suger, redesigning St Denis, Paris, pioneered the soaring, lofty architecture of the Gothic style, with its high vaulting reaching up to heaven. He wanted to move viewers "from the material to the immaterial" that they may be "translated by divine grace from the inferior to a higher

---

1. Ramsey, *Glory of God*, 147.
2. Wright, *Early History of Heaven*.

world."³ This contrasts with stocky Romanesque buildings which, with their heavy thick walls, seem more connected to the earth!

Paul expresses the dilemma well:

> This one thing I do: forgetting what lies behind and straining forward to what lies ahead, I press on toward the goal for the prize of the heavenly [upward] call of God in Christ Jesus. . . .Our citizenship is in heaven, and it is from there that we are expecting a Savior, the Lord Jesus Christ. He will transform the body of our humiliation that it may be conformed to the body of his glory. . . (Phil 3:12–14, 20–21)

Paul is clear: "our homeland is in heaven" (Phil 4:20, TLB).

Here below we are, as 1 Peter 2:21 puts it, in various translations:

- sojourners and exiles (ESV)
- aliens and temporary residents (CJB)
- strangers and pilgrims (AV)
- Dear friends, your real home is not here on earth (NLV)
- Brothers and sisters, you are only visitors here since your real home is in heaven (TLB)

The writer to the Colossians is emphatic:

> If then you have been raised with Christ, seek the things that are above, where Christ is, seated at the right hand of God. Set your minds on things that are above, not on things that are on earth. (Col 3:1–3)

How Does The Transfiguration Express This Paradox?

The Transfiguration event occurs at a point where heaven and earth intersect. Tabor stands at the threshold of heaven and at the brink of eternity.

The Church Fathers noted the significance of Moses and Elijah in the company of the disciples. Timothy of Antioch (7th cent.) asks:

> Why was it these three, and those two? That the saying of Paul might be fulfilled, "In the name of Jesus every knee will bend of those in heaven, on earth and under the earth." From those under

---

3. David Brown, quoted by Harries, "Meanings".

the earth [in burial] he led Moses up; from those in heaven he brought Elijah down [who ascended in a chariot]; from those on the earth he established Peter and James and John.[4]

Or as Leontius of Constantinople (6th cent.) puts it bluntly:

> He lured Elijah down from above. He fished Moses up from below, he set Peter and James and John alongside him from those still on earth: for the whole is known from the extremes![5]

In the figures of the two Hebrew figures and the three disciples gathered around Jesus, the whole universe comes together, and heaven and earth touch!

This is symbolized most poignantly in Matthew's account:

> The disciples fell on their faces to the ground, and were filled with awe. But Jesus came and touched them, saying, "Rise, and have no fear." And when they lifted up their eyes, they saw no one but Jesus only. (Matt 17: 6–8, RSV).

The disciples have their faces in the dust of the earth; then they are lifted up by the radiant Jesus. But the whole story is set within this dynamic and tension between earth and heaven, because it is a transcendent episode set within a long and dusty journey.

THE SETTING OF THE TRANSFIGURATION

The gospels give us an itinerary: before approaching the mountain, Jesus travels through Nazareth, Capernaum, Tyre and Sidon in the far north, the Decapolis region east of the Jordan, Bethsaida on the lake's northern shore; Caesarea Philippi.

Galilee of the Gentiles

Matthew's gospel quotes Isaiah (9:1,2) at the very start of this account of the ministry, anticipating the setting of Transfiguration and showing the context chosen by Jesus:

---

4. Daley, *Light on the Mountain*, 150.
5. Daley, *Light on the Mountain*, 126.

> Land of Zebulun, land of Naphtali,
> On the road by the sea, across the Jordan,
> Galilee of the Gentiles –
> People who sat in darkness have seen a great light ... (Matt 5:15)

"Galilee of the Gentiles"—the phrase means literally: "circle of pagans." The Galilee region was much more mixed in terms of Jewish and Gentile populations than other regions of the land. A semi-autonomous frontier region, it was exposed to the nearby foreign countries and ethnicities. Studies by Horsley and Freyne illuminate for us the marginality of Galilee.[6] Freyne calls Galilee "a symbol of the periphery becoming the new non-localized center of divine presence."[7] It maintained both a physical distance from the Temple on Zion and an ideological distance, prepared to make a critique of the self-serving Jerusalem clerical elite and their practices. It found itself on the edges. Galileans were mocked for their local accent—recall the girl's recognition of Peter's rough Aramaic tongue—they were jeered at and scapegoated. "Can anything good come out of Nazareth?" asks Nathaniel (John 1:46). "Search and you will see that no prophet is to arise from Galilee" (John 7:52). Lee observes:

> Galileans were not just left alone in their liminal situation but were oppressed, dehumanized and looked down upon. Galileans were marginalized by foreign invaders and also by the Jerusalem Temple-state ... Galilee was repeatedly invaded and exploited by foreign empires throughout its history.[8]

But above all, it was a place of deep poverty and need. The Galileans were crippled by heavy taxes, dues were owed to the Roman occupier, and Temple taxes added to the burden. At the time of Jesus ordinary families were being forced to quit their ancestral landholdings, where they had lived for centuries, in order to meet these demands. Land was also confiscated for the building projects and villas of the urban elite at Sefforis and Tiberias. But then they had to pay rent for what had been their fields and homes: caught in a downwards economic spiral, becoming tenants in their own property.[9] Tax and rent robbed the Galilean peasant farmer of two thirds of the family income. Many were living at barely subsistence level.

---

6. Freyne, *Jesus, A Jewish Galilean*; Horsley, *Archaeology, History and Society*.

7. Freyne, *Galilee, Jesus and the Gospels*, 54.

8. Lee, *From a Liminal Place*, 47.

9. Note how many of Jesus' parables speak of absentee landlords imposing severe dues on their tenants (see, for example, Luke 16:1–8; Matt 25:14–30).

No doubt Matthew preserves an original aspect of the Lord's Prayer when he puts it: "Forgive us our debts and we forgive those who are in debt to us" (Matt 6:12). Jesus asks his disciples to pray for the coming of God's Kingdom: a subversive prayer when taught and uttered in the context of first century Galilee, for it embodies a challenge to the prevailing kingdom, the kingdom of Rome, the rule of the Caesar. But this imperial reign had become stiflingly oppressive for the Galilean. The area of Galilee became a base for resistance to Rome's occupation: indeed, Josephus tells us, the seedbed of the Zealots, revolutionary activists undermining Roman domination by acts of sabotage or terrorism. Where there is oppression amidst powerlessness, one reaction is the rise of violent terrorists or guerrilla fighters. Ever since the uprising by Judas the Galilean in 4BC, Galilee was infamous for these protesters and rebels.

A liminal place, land that is betwixt and between, caught between foreign countries and the religious center, a place experiencing oppression, woundedness and protest: this is the earthly setting of the transcendent Transfiguration.

HEAVEN ON EARTH

In the course of his journeys through Galilee, we get glimpses into the earthy Jesus. He pauses to notice the details of how things grow, or not, in the soils by the Sea of Galilee (parable of the Sower, Mark 4). He celebrates how the Kingdom of God is revealed in the earth producing seed (4:26). He feels the spray and wetness of the storm on the lake (Mark 6). He is very much in touch with the natural world.

In Matthew 13, as we noted, Jesus tells us that the "secrets of the kingdom of heaven" (13:11, in Greek "the Kingdom of the Heavens") are hidden beneath our very feet. They are to be found in the ground. The Kingdom of Heaven is glimpsed in seed planted in the earth (vv. 3, 24), mustard placed in soil (v.31), treasure hidden in a field (v.44). If we want to discover the Kingdom of Heaven we start by looking down, attending to the earth beneath us!

And not only the earth itself—Jesus' Kingdom of God was this-worldly, concerned about how men and women treat each other in human society.

Scholars point out that the one subject most likely to lead to conflict with the Roman authorities is the question of rule—and Jesus frames his message precisely around the concept of the reign of God: what would life look like if God, not Caesar, were on the throne?[10] Jesus challenges both the power of Rome and the conventions of first century Judaism by his message about the Kingdom of God, where all are welcome and all are equal. The Kingdom of God represents a new way of living, a different path, an alternative vision for society, and the Sermon on the Mount reads like a radical manifesto.

Jesus did not want to be a conquering hero vanquishing Rome by might. He did not come to lead a political revolution but rather to call members of society back being to a covenantal egalitarian community, marked by respect for one another—calling human society back to Mosaic covenantal cooperation and mutuality.[11] As New Testament scholar Stephen Need puts it: "It is clear that Jesus did not think of the kingdom of God as lying in the future or in the other world. Nor did he see it as an individual, personal or spiritual thing. He saw the kingdom as God's rule for the whole of creation bringing about a new age in which all people would be included. Jesus' teaching, preaching and healing concerned a physical, tangible this-worldly reality affecting everyone. . .it concerned life as actually lived, communities as they relate to each other and societies as they treat each other."[12]

But we are permitted—at the same time as we attend to such earthly concerns—to lift our gaze heavenwards, for the Transfiguration episode is introduced by these words: "Truly, I say to you, there are some standing here who will not taste death before they see the kingdom of God come with power."

We may not only glimpse the Kingdom of God in glimpses of heaven—in what Matthew calls an *orama* or vision[13]—we may also glimpse God's reign here below.

BORDERLANDS

Drawn to the Mountains

We see that Jesus appreciates very much the dust and soil of the earth, and the contours of the landscape. But he is drawn, irresistibly, decisively, to

---

10. This phrase derives from Crossan, *Revolutionary Biography*.
11. Horsley, *Jesus and Empire; Prophet Jesus*.
12. Need, *Following Jesus*, 57.
13. Giving us the word pan-orama, Matt 17:9.

mountains: "Six days later, Jesus took with him Peter and James and John, and led them up a high mountain apart, by themselves" (Mark 9:2).

In his important study *Jesus on the Mountain* Terence Donaldson notices that Matthew mentions Jesus ascending no less than six different mountains.[14] For his part, Luke points out that Jesus ascends mountains in order to pray and to discern:

> Now during those days he went out to the mountain to pray; and he spent the night in prayer to God. And when day came, he called his disciples and chose twelve of them, whom he also named apostles. (Luke 6:12,13)

Luke also gives us the impression that Jesus ascended that mountain to gain some space for two things: space in which to prepare himself for a demanding ministry of healing, and space in which to clarify his message, for the account goes on:

> He came down with them and stood on a level place, with a great crowd of his disciples and a great multitude of people from all Judea, Jerusalem, and the coast of Tyre and Sidon. They had come to hear him and to be healed of their diseases; and those who were troubled with unclean spirits were cured. And all in the crowd were trying to touch him, for power came out from him and healed all of them. Then he looked up at his disciples and said: "Blessed are you who are poor, for yours is the kingdom of God." (Luke 6:17–20)

Hermon or Tabor ?

Which mountain of Transfiguration did Jesus actually climb?

Mount Hermon with its icy peaks piercing the blue firmament above broods over Upper Galilee. Towering ten thousand feet above sea-level and with its close proximity to Caesarea Philippi, the previous scene in the gospel accounts, most scholars agree that this is the most likely locale for the awesome event we call the Transfiguration. It resonates most clearly with Mark's description of "a high mountain apart" (Mark 9:2). Mount Hermon is part of the Anti-Lebanon range of mountains and dominates the area. Stunningly snow-capped for much of the year, clouds enshrouding

14. Mount of Temptation (4); Mountain of the Sermon (5–7); Mountain of healing (15); Mount of Transfiguration (17); Mount of eschatological discourse (24, 25); Mountain of the Great Commission (28). Donaldson, *Jesus on the Mountain*.

its peaks, it evokes Matthew's observation, "His clothing was as white as snow." Meltwaters from the snow form the origins of the River Jordan, which streams forth at its feet at Banias. The mountain is steeply-sided, and it is a hard climb to make an ascent into its beauty and mystery. The Bible celebrates the cascading dew of Mount Hermon (Ps 133:3) and suggests it might be a dangerous place, with its "dens of lions . . . mountains of leopards" (Song 4:8)!

In the Bible Mount Hermon denotes the northern boundary of the Transjordan, the edge of the Amorite territory, and it marks the border to the terrain associated with the tribe of Manasseh. Today the mountain is a borderland in a political sense: here the countries of Lebanon, Syria and Israel meet.

However, the pilgrim and liturgical tradition, since the fourth century, favors Tabor as the mount of Transfiguration.

Mount Tabor rises mysteriously and majestically in Lower Galilee, an intriguing oval shape, above the Plain of Jezreel. Its thickly-wooded sides, fragrant with pine, seem to point up to heaven itself. It is exposed to the elements, and often shrouded in low mist or cloud.

> As I live, says the King, whose name is the Lord of hosts,
> one is coming like Tabor among the mountains. (Jer 46:18)

It is pre-eminently a place of beauty with its other-worldly shape, two thousand feet above the Plain. Its transcendent quality accounts for its identification by the Byzantines as the place of the Transfiguration and in this book we shall use the designation Tabor as a short-hand for the place of this mystery.

A Liminal Place

The mountain of Transfiguration becomes a spiritual borderland, a place of transition where sky meets soil, where glory and passion mingle. Jesus takes his disciples to a sublimely liminal place, the edge of heaven, the brink of eternity. The barrier between heaven and earth is breached, as two worlds meet. The barriers of time are dissolved, as Moses and Elijah appear with Jesus, and the past encounters the present, embracing the future. Mortality and immortality interpenetrate in the radiant person of Christ. The Divine reveals itself in the human, and physicality of Christ's body shines with immaterial light. The mountain turns out to be a place of breakthrough, a watershed in the gospel accounts, a pivotal moment, pointing to another mountain, Calvary. But it is an unpredictable place. One minute the disciples are incandescent with divine light and the next they are soaked in a wet fog. As Hebrews (12:26) puts it: "When God spoke from Mount Sinai his voice shook the earth, but now he makes another promise: 'Once again I will shake not only the earth but the heavens also.'"

Divine Light upon the Stones

Let's see what light the Orthodox Church can shine on this paradox—because the Transfiguration is one of its greatest feasts. Kallistos Ware reminds us: "The Transfiguration shows us how material things—not only Christ's face, hands and feet, but also his clothes; and not only the body of Christ, but also those of the three disciples upon whom the rays of light fall; and not they alone, but likewise the grass, trees, flowers and rocks of the mountainside which also share in the radiance that emanates from Christ—all these can be transformed, rendered luminous, filled with translucence and glory. The Transfiguration reveals the Spirit-bearing potentialities of all material things."[15]

In fact all Orthodox icon painters (writers) are required to begin their training by crafting an icon of the Transfiguration. Metropolitan Anthony Bloom encountered in Moscow the two greatest icons of the Transfiguration, those of Andrei Rublev (1360–1430) and Theophan the Greek (1340–1410), noting:

> The Rublev icon shows Christ in the brilliancy of His dazzling white robes which cast light on everything around. The light falls on the disciples, on the mountains and the stones, on every blade of grass. Within this light, which is the divine glory, the divine light itself inseparable from God, all things acquire an intensity of being which they could not have otherwise; in it they attain to a fulness of reality which they can have only in God.
>
> In the work by Theophan the Greek we discover all these rays of light falling from the Divine Presence. . .touch things and sink into them, penetrate them, touch something within them so that from the core of all things created, the same light reflects and shines back as though the divine life quickens the capabilities, the potentialities, of all things. . .in the words of St Paul, "God is all in all."[16]

15. Ware, "Safeguarding the Creation".
16. Quoted in Ware, *Inner Kingdom*, 108. Theophan was the teacher of Rublev: in the

In his icon Theophan the Greek paints the disciples and the mountain in dirty, earthy colors, greens and browns. Despite the supernatural nature of the scene Theophan wants us to remember that the Transfiguration is truly happening on earth. The white and heavenly blue scattered over the surfaces of mountain and men indicate that eternal heaven has come down to this place at this specific time. Heaven is gilding earth. Through the blue lines emanating from Jesus to his friends' eyes we understand that heaven is being revealed to them. As Dionysius testifies: "This light reaches to the smallest and most remote parts of creation completely undiminished, unifies the creation and draws the creation back to the Creator."[17]

Both icons declare that the divine light touches and transforms the earth. The radiant aureole illuminates the cosmos. The Transfiguration explodes with seismic implications, like a volcanic eruption, spreading divine flame over the earth: "I have come to cast fire upon the earth" (Luke 12:49). It evokes the prayer of Habakkuk:

> Lord, I have heard the report of what you did;
> I am awed, Lord, by what you accomplished.
> In our time repeat those deeds;
> in our time reveal them again.
> God comes from Teman,
> the Holy One from Mount Paran.
> His splendor has covered the skies,
> the earth is full of his glory.
> His brightness will be as lightning. (Hab 3:1–4, NET)

THE RENEWAL OF ALL CREATION

> O God, who in Your goodness have sanctified with Your light
> all the inhabited earth,
> You were transfigured upon a high mountain,
> showing Your might to Your disciples: For You redeem the world.[18]

The Transfiguration has very clear links with the baptism of Christ. At the Jordan the Father's voice is heard in a similar affirmation: "A voice came from heaven, 'You are my beloved Son, with you I am well-pleased'" (Mark

---

beginning, the two were master and student; later, they became collaborators.

17. Andreaopoulos, *Metamorphosis*, 148.
18. Mother Mary and Ware, *Festal Menaion*, 474.

1:11). Before we turn to Orthodox liturgical texts for the Transfiguration to explore an emphasis on creation, we first revisit the truth celebrated in the Feast of Theophany: in the coming of Jesus to the Jordan we see the entry of the divine Creator Word, the creator Word made flesh (John 1:18) into the very midst of creation, as the deep and powerful currents of the Jordan swirl around him. At the self-same moment as the naked body of the incarnate creator Word is submerged, enveloped, inundated by the waters, the divine Spirit descends, in an echo from Genesis 1:2 "The earth was complete chaos, and darkness covered the face of the deep, while a wind from God swept over the face of the waters."

The early Church fathers noted its significance. Cyril of Alexandria (376–444), in his commentary on Matthew 3 declares: "Christ was not baptized as one repenting but as one sanctifying the waters" (Fragment 29, *Stromateis*). Saint Maximos of Turin (380–420) puts it: "Christ is baptized, not to be made holy by the water, but to make the water holy, and by his cleansing to purify the waters which he touched. For the consecration of Christ involves a more significant consecration of the water. For when the Savior is washed all water is made clean, purified at its source for the dispensing of baptismal grace to the people of future ages."[19]

Professor Ioannes Fountoulis explains:

> First, as the beginning and the head of the new people, Christ is baptized and sanctifies the created waters to create through them the new world, the New Creation, new people, faithful Christbearers and Godbearers. In the celebration of the Theophany, after the blessing of the water and the communion and the sprinkling of believers, the catechumens were baptized. It was the feast of "the Lights". The "illumination"—the baptism of Christ and Christians.[20]

Christ by his baptism sanctifies this water and makes it the means, not only of our healing by partaking of it, but of the renewal of the creation. The entire planet is sanctified by means of Christ's baptism, beginning with that most basic element of creation—water. It was the mystical waters that were separated to form the heavens and the earth. So, with the sanctification of water, all creation becomes good, pure again; it becomes what it first was, it returns to its first beauty. It takes on a "spiritual" quality, renewed as a means of communicating God's grace. Elizabeth Scalia puts it:

19. Maximos of Turin, "Sermon 100".
20. Fountoulis, "Theophany".

With Christ's baptism, God no longer moved upon the face of the water, he was immersed within it—and not thoughtlessly, as a child playing in a river, but God-mindfully; with an intention to save. The whole body of Christ Jesus, intentionally submerged by John (by Christ's command), enhanced and perhaps exceeded creation; rather than God's Spirit moving upon the face of things, God Incarnate—*Emmanuel*—sanctified the water with his very flesh. And the water flowed, and it fed streams and animals and plants, and it rose, and it fell and it renewed the face of the earth in the most mystical of ways, because it was now, and forever more, *holy* water—literally touched by God, with an intention full of love and mercy. God particles, multiplied into infinity, and all around us, contained in all that grows and flows.[21]

Blessing the Waters of Creation

"Christ has shone forth in the Jordan to sanctify the waters." The Orthodox celebration of the Baptism of Christ in the feast of the Theophany is no mere recalling of an historical event but rather a celebration of present reality. It reaches its climax with the ceremony of the Blessing of the Waters, taking place at a local river or around a font or bowl of water placed in the center of the church building. Surrounded by candles and flowers, this water stands for the beautiful world of God's original creation and ultimate glorification by Christ in the Kingdom of God, and this hymn is sung:

> Let us the faithful praise the greatness of God's plan for us.
> For He Who alone is pure and undefiled
> becomes a man because of our transgressions.
> He is cleansed with our cleansing in the Jordan,
> sanctifying both us and the waters,
> and crushing the heads of the dragons in the water.
> Therefore, let us draw water in gladness,
> for upon those who draw in faith
> the grace of the Spirit is invisibly bestowed by Christ God,
> the Savior of our souls.[22]

This hymn expresses the thought-world of the Ancient Near East, where the waters of sea or river were feared as the abode of chaos. The waters are brimming with demons and monsters. We even know their names! Here

21. Scalia, "Christ is baptized".
22. Orthodox Church in America.

lurks Leviathan and Rahab (Ps 74:13–14). As the priest holds a wooden cross in his hands, to be cast upon the face of the waters, this great hymn by Sophronios, Patriarch of Jerusalem is sung:

> The voice of the Lord is upon the waters crying:
> "Come, one and all, receive the Spirit of wisdom. . ."
> Today the nature of the waters is sanctified!

This celebration, uniquely, draws us to a key meaning hidden in the event of the baptism of Christ in the Jordan. The entry of the Word into the center of creation reconsecrates creation, and declares the natural world sacred, to be treated with reverence, because it is infused with the Divine—indeed it is God-bearing, God-revealing, an Epiphany, Theophany, a veritable sacrament. Alexander Schmemann sums it up in the title of his great book *The World as Sacrament*:

> What is important for us is that the baptismal water represents the matter of the cosmos, the world as life of humanity. Its blessing acquires thus a cosmic and redemptive significance. God created the world and blessed it and gave it to humanity as food and life, as a means of communion with him. The blessing of the water signifies the return or redemption of matter to this initial and essential meaning. By accepting the baptism of John, Christ sanctified the water—made it the water of purification and reconciliation with God. It was then, as Christ was coming out of the water, that the Epiphany—the new and redemptive manifestation of God—took place, and the Spirit of God, who at the beginning of creation "moved upon the face of the waters", made water—that is, the world—again into what he made them at the beginning. . .Once more the world is proclaimed to be what Christ revealed and made it to be—the gift of God to humanity, the means of humanity's communion with God. . .Faith in Christ that leads a person to baptism today is precisely the certitude that Christ is the only true "content"—meaning, being and end—of all that exists, the fulness of him who fills all things. In faith the whole world becomes the sacrament of his presence, the means of life in him. And water, the image and presence of the world, is truly the image and presence of Christ.[23]

---

23. Schmemann, *World as Sacrament*, 88–90.

Blessing the Fruits of the Earth

The Orthodox liturgy for Theophany anticipates the theme of the renewal of creation, developed in its texts for the Feast of the Transfiguration:

> Today all things are filled with joy,
> for Christ is transfigured before the Disciples.
> In Your goodness You have sanctified the whole world with Your Light.

Symeon the New Theologian speaks of sanctifying the temple of the world:

> When man finds his destiny, which is to glorify God,
> he also leads the whole of creation to its destiny, which is to glorify God.
> As he sanctifies the temple of his being,
> man also sanctifies the temple of the entire world.
> Thus he transforms creation,
> making it sing the praises of the divine Majesty.[24]

The liturgical blessing of grapes, as well as other fruits and vegetables on this day is a beautiful sign of the final transfiguration of all things in Christ. It signifies the ultimate flowering and fruitfulness of all creation in the paradise of God's unending Kingdom of Life where all will be transformed by the glory of the Lord. Professor Panagiotis Skaltsis explains:

> With the Transfiguration of the Lord the whole world is illumined and glorified. Creation is exhilarated and acquires the brilliance that creation at one time had . . . The blessing of the grapes, representing the harvest of the world, is a liturgical act that emphasizes the doxological and Eucharistic offering of the material and the fruits of the earth to the Creator and God of all things. More so, when this fruit of the vine gives us wine, which Christ blessed in Cana, to show the Transfiguration of the world in Christ. For this reason creation responds with thanksgiving for this gift and this hope. It references its Creator and thanks Him, and the Church, in the most appropriate feast, blesses the world and the harvest, Creation and the Eschaton, with renewal and hope. The renewal that begins with God, and passes through nature, leads to the salvation of humanity.[25]

Back in the seventh century, the abbot Anastasius of the monastery of Sinai had exalted:

---

24. Kesolopoulos, *Environment*, 66.
25. Skaltsis, "Why Do We Bless Grapes".

> Creation rejoiced when it heard [on Tabor] of its transformation from corruption to incorruptibility; the mountain was filled with delight, the fields were joyful; the sea chanted hymns, the rivers clapped their hands; the hills leapt; the deserts bloomed; all things were unified, all things were filled with joy.[26]

RENEWED COMMITMENTS

The seemingly other-worldly event of the Transfiguration leads us to a fresh commitment to care for the mountains and rivers, indeed for the whole of creation. We respond to the Transfiguration by blessing the earth. The rays of divine light emanating from the transfigured Christ reach out to embrace and penetrate the whole cosmos. Glimpsing heaven, our ultimate homeland, we become more resolved than ever to appreciate the earthly paradise. As the Ecumenical Patriarch has said recently:

> The Lord suffuses all of creation with His divine presence in one continuous legato from the substance of the atoms to the Mind of God. Let us renew the harmony between heaven and earth, and transfigure every detail, every particle of life. Let us love one another, and lovingly learn from one another, for the edification of God's people, for the sanctification of God's creation, and for the glorification of God's most holy Name.[27]

Orthodox Andrew Vincent Rossi asks:

> If the transfiguration of creation appears to be too impractical, or "out of this world," or too unrealistic a notion to have any real meaning or impact in our daily lives, how should we raise ourselves up so that the doctrine of the transfiguration of creation becomes comprehensible? How can we understand it so that it makes a difference in the actions and decisions we make in our daily lives? How can we get our minds around it so that it might influence our hearts, and be a lamp unto our feet and a light unto our path (Ps 119:105)?
>
> The most important thing of all is to instill in our minds by every means possible that the loving care for creation is an absolute requirement placed by the Triune God on all humanity... the command written into human nature by God at the creation to

---

26. Daley, *Light on The Mountain*, 176.
27. Bartholomew, "Presentation to Metropolitan Nikitas".

love and care for creation means ultimately that human beings are to participate in the transfiguration of creation.

The Transfiguration of Christ breaches the three primary boundaries of created existence, space, time and matter: Divine infinity transfiguring space, eternity transfiguring time, and limitless, uncreated light transfiguring matter. The cosmos itself is torn open and transfigured by the power of the Triune God revealed in these climactic moments in the life of Christ. The boundary is between the Divine and the human, the uncreated and the created, eternity and time, the heaven and the earth, death in life, and life in death. Christ's life is thus revealed as the paradigm of spiritual initiation, transformation and transfiguration, a paradigm that includes not only the Divine and the human, but all created nature. This is the witness of the Gospels.[28]

The Letter to the Ephesians puts it:

> God has made known to us the mystery of his will,
> according to his good pleasure that he set forth in Christ,
> as a plan for the fullness of time,
> to gather up all things in him,
> things in heaven and things on earth. (Eph 1:9,10)

To live the transfigured life between earth and heaven, we rediscover the paradox that the Kingdom of Heaven is beneath our feet. As Michael Ramsey put it:

> A gospel of transfiguration transcends the world and yet speaks directly to the immediate here-and-now. He who is transfigured is the Son of Man; and as he discloses on the holy mountain another world, he reveals that no part of created things, and no moment of created time lies outside the power of the Spirit, who is Lord, to change it from glory to glory.[29]

WHAT LAND IS HOLY?

The "Holy Land" reveals in a poignant way the paradox. The very name evokes images of terrain graced by the presence and revelation of God, a land of "holy places" where we can encounter God powerfully. But the "Holy Land" becomes a place of contradiction and ambiguity today: is it

28. Rossi, "The Transfiguration of Creation".
29. Ramsey, *Glory of God*, 147.

made unholy by humans inflicting here various types of oppressions? Some even refuse to call it the "Holy Land", preferring instead the designation "the Land of the Holy One." So, what is holiness: how do we recognize it? What *is* a holy place? These are crucial issues for all Christians, whether pilgrims to the Holy Land or those living as pilgrims at home. What is holy? Where, indeed, do we find God?

Behind the word "holy", the root meaning of the Hebrew *qadesh* is to separate, to set apart. It refers, first of all, to God as utterly Other, transcendent, with a vast gap between Creator and creature. People or places consecrated to God become holy: "Be holy, as I am holy" (1 Pet 1:16; Lev 11:44). Mount Tabor developed as a designated "holy place" in the wake of the Emperor Constantine's conversion in the fourth century and the visit of his mother Helena to this land to identify sites associated with Christ. Splendid Byzantine churches marked these out as sites for worship and pilgrimage. Many became what the Celtic tradition calls "thin places", where any barrier between heaven and earth, between the human and divine is easily crossed—where there is often, to this day, a palpable sense of God's presence, deepened by the prayers of the centuries in these holy places. Here pilgrims sense what Otto called "the numinous" in his classic work *A Sense of the Holy*.

But the singular Mount Tabor reminds us that the Divine touches and sanctifies earth everywhere on the planet: every square inch is sacred and worthy of reverence and respect. The light of the transfigured Christ shines on the rocks and earth. Holiness is no longer about separation. It is contagious! The Incarnation overturns the traditional dichotomy between sacred and secular, the divide between "holy" and "unholy." It challenges us to glimpse the Divine in the dust, and to be alert to God's presence throughout our broken planet. All the earth is sacred, and all who dwell therein. As Orthodox theologian Dumitri Stăniloae puts it: "God sparkles from everything."[30]

QUESTIONS FOR REFLECTION

1. How do you live out the paradox of living each day committed to earthly tasks while at the same time holding the hope of heaven and nurturing a divine perspective on things?

---

30. Stăniloae, *Orthodox Spirituality*, 209.

2. What part do you see for yourself in the renewal of creation through ecology and care of the planet?

3. How do you respond to the claim: "Through our creative powers, through science, technology, craftsmanship and art, we enlarge the radiance of the transfigured Christ, revealing in all material things the glory that is latent within them"?[31]

4. We saw how the liturgies for the Baptism of Christ and Transfiguration speak of the sanctification of the world. How does it work out in practice—to see the earth beneath your feet as holy, or streets, for example, as God-bearing, sacred ground? Does this make any difference to the way you go about?

5. How do you find yourselves responding to this scripture: "Then [on Sinai] his voice shook the earth, but now he promises: 'Yet once more I shake not only the earth, but also heaven.' This means that in this final shaking all that is impermanent will be removed, that is, everything that is merely made, and only the unshakeable things will remain. Since then we have been given a Kingdom that is unshakeable, let us serve God with thankfulness in the ways which please him, but always with reverence and holy fear" (Heb 12:26–29, Phillips).

PRAYER EXERCISE

This prayer time is in three parts.
First, recall the thin places of your own life.
The Transfiguration mountain became for Peter, James and John what the Celtic tradition calls a "thin place"—parting the veil between this world and the other world, between heaven and earth, between the Divine and the human, between matter and spirit, between the eternal and the temporal. In the thin place the duality of those parings disappears: we encounter a palpable sense of the Divine.

Recall a time that the veil parted for you and you knew that you not only stood in the presence of the Holy but you experienced a sense of closeness with God. Remember—fusing memory and imagination—and give thanks to God for his presence at different times and seasons of your life. Use the words of the psalm:

---

31. Ware, "Safeguarding the Creation".

> I will call to mind the deeds of the Lord;
> I will remember your wonders of old.
> I will meditate on all your work, and muse on your mighty deeds.
> Your way, O God, is holy. What god is so great as our God?
> You are the God who works wonders;
> You display your might among the peoples. (Ps 77:11–14)

Secondly, look around you—or call to mind—your normal context, setting and community. Let some of the local needs or challenges enter your consciousness. Picture your rural or urban landscape that conceals many needs. See the sun rising on them—batheing them in the transfiguring light of Christ. Pray slowly:

> I am listening carefully to all the Lord is saying—
> for he speaks peace to his people.
> Surely his salvation is near to those who reverence him;
> our land will be filled with his glory.
> Mercy and truth have met together. Justice and peace have kissed!
> Truth rises from the earth,
> and righteousness smiles down from heaven.
> Yes, the Lord pours down his blessings on the land:
> it yields bountiful crops.
> Justice goes before him to make a pathway for his steps.
> (Ps 85: 8–12, LB)

Thirdly, conclude with a prayer of yearning. With longing and desiring, ask God for the grace to open up "thin places" in your daily life.

> As a deer longs for flowing streams,
> so my soul longs for you, O God.
> My soul thirsts for God, for the living God.
> When shall I come and behold the face of God? (Ps 42)

Michael Marsh puts it:

> The Transfiguration is not simply a story about Peter, James, and John. It is descriptive of Christ's encounter with all humanity. We too are called to the thin places. We too are invited to step through the parted veil. Transfiguration is all around us. Jesus is always leading us to the thin places of our life.[32]

Or

Meditate on John Keble's hymn that declares "Two worlds are ours."

---

32. Marsh, "Thin Places, Veils, and Transfiguration".

> There is a book who runs may read, Which heavenly truth imparts,
> And all the lore its scholars need Pure eyes and loving hearts.
>
> The glorious sky, embracing all, Is like the Maker's love,
> Wherewith encompassed, great and small
> In peace and order move.
>
> One Name, above all glorious names,
> With its ten thousand tongues
> The everlasting sea proclaims, Echoing angelic songs.
>
> The raging fire, the roaring wind, His boundless power display;
> And in the gentler breeze we find His Spirit's viewless way.
>
> Two worlds are ours; and ours to win The wisdom to descry
> The mystic heaven and earth within, Plain as the sea and sky.
>
> Thou who hast given me eyes to see And love this sight so fair,
> Give me a heart to find out thee, And read thee everywhere!

Keble pens in his hymn "New Every Morning is the Love"

> If on our daily course our mind be set to hallow all we find,
> new treasures still, of countless price, God will provide for sacrifice.
> The trivial round, the common task, will furnish all we need to ask,
> room to deny ourselves, a road to bring us daily nearer God.

End with the prayer

> *O God, the protector of all who trust in you,*
> *without whom nothing is strong, nothing is holy:*
> *increase and multiply upon us your mercy;*
> *that with you as our ruler and guide*
> *we may so pass through things temporal*
> *that we lose not our hold on things eternal;*
> *Through Jesus Christ our Lord, Amen.*

Icon of the Transfiguration by Theophan the Greek, 1408

2

Flourishing
Between Humanity and Divinity

A RAW, VISCERAL IMAGE presents itself: Jesus, glistening in sweat dripping from his forehead in the heat of the sun and in the exertion of the climb up Tabor's steep slopes—a very human Jesus, exhausted, vulnerable.

But now: shimmering in light—a luminous vision confronts us: Jesus, incandescent, aglow and dazzling in beauty.

A shining—first with very human perspiration, second with divinity!

And, atop the mountain, this same Jesus, before whom the disciples fall on their faces in fear and awe, a transcendent Christ whose face "shone like the sun"—now reveals a heart of great tenderness and gentle compassion as he draws close to them on the ground, touches them with his hands, and helps them arise: transcendence meets tenderness, ultimacy embraces intimacy, majesty enfolds meekness, Otherness becomes immanence, overshadowing transmutes into undergirding:

> He was transfigured before them. His face shone like the sun, and his clothes became as white as the light.
> When the disciples heard the voice, they fell face down to the ground, terrified.
> But Jesus came and touched them. "Get up," he said. "Don't be afraid." (Matt 17:2,6,7)

It is a poignant and moving scene. We notice that Jesus takes the initiative—he approaches them in their distress.[1] He touches them. Elsewhere in Matthew Jesus' touch is for healing and restoration.[2] Here we see also reassuring solidarity that declares: "I am one with you. I understand what you are feeling."

EXPERIENCING OUR MORTALITY

The disciples with face to the ground become a powerful symbol of humanity in its fallenness. At one moment, the radiant Jesus seems totally Other, and in the next he is enfolding the disciples in their confusion and incredulity. He meets them in their vulnerability and brokenness, and calls them from bewilderment to a new sense of their vocation and identity. From having their faces in the earth, they stand upright, lifted up and elevated by Jesus, and gain a fresh sense of composure and dignity. In his strong arms and gentle hands, Jesus raises them up from their abasement and sets their feet on a new road. With their faces in the dust of the earth, they are returning to their origins, to the earth from which they are made (Gen 2:7), but Jesus lifts them up into a new creation. "Arise!" It is, indeed, a forestate of resurrection! We see two paradoxes here: Jesus is both Other and near; the disciples are fallen yet called to a new destiny. Humanity meets divinity.

We live in a time when people's self-worth has been severely undermined by a range of factors: the ravages of pandemic, the interminable comparing of ourselves with others through social media. Our self-image and understanding of ourselves has become eroded. We are more conscious than ever before of human mortality, vulnerability, finitude, weakness. Horrifyingly, suicide rates among young men are soaring and instances of self-harm increasing. Many become demoralized and depressed, gloomy and pessimistic about the human condition. We can feel battered and bruised by life, and healthy self-esteem fades away. Mount Tabor beckons us: we can glimpse again an awesome and inspiring view of our very purpose and being.

Tabor opens before us the opportunity to see the glory and potentiality in each person rather than only seeing weakness and doom. Tabor teaches us about honoring our personhood. Tabor restores our dignity, our identity, our very sense of purpose: revealing divine invincibility within human frailty!

1. As on the mount of the great commission, Matt 28:18.
2. Matt 8:3,15; 9:20,29; 14:36; 20:34.

DISCOVERING OUR IMMORTALITY

Wake Up to Who You Really Are!

Luke suggests that the prayer experience of the Transfiguration is a place of awakening, heightened consciousness and alert awareness. First we read: "Now Peter and his companions were weighed down with sleep"—as the same three disciples will show us in Gethsemane, they are quick to succumb to fatigue, exhaustion, sleep. They epitomize human frailty.

The account goes straight on: "but becoming fully awake, they saw his glory" (9:32) The disciples become awakened, dazzled, awestruck. They will never be the same again. They are invited to a wakefulness in which their spiritual senses are put on high alert. They are invited to *look*: to gaze on the mystery, to open their eyes to the light. They are invited to open their ears and *hear*: the Father's voice, from heaven, calls out: "Listen to him!" They are *touched*: the moisture of the wet mist soaks their skin, and Jesus reaches out his hands to them to touch them and lift them up. There is an awakening of the spirit and the body: a coming fully-alive, aware and responsive to what God wanted to offer them.

It is the disciples too who become transfigured, changed! *They* experience *metamorphosis*. They are, literally, being re-arranged, their lives becoming reshaped. It is significant that while the Gospels use this word—which we transliterate as "transfigure"—only for Jesus, Paul uses the word only for Christian disciples!

> Do not conform to the pattern of this world, but be transfigured by the renewing of your mind. (Rom 12:2)

> All of us who are Christians have no veils on our faces, but reflect like mirrors the glory of the Lord. We are transfigured by the Spirit of the Lord in ever-increasing splendor into his own image. (2 Cor 3:18, Phillips)

> All of us, as with unveiled face, because we continue to behold as in a mirror the glory of the Lord, are constantly being transfigured into His very own image in ever increasing splendor and from one degree of glory to another; this comes from the Lord Who is the Spirit. (2 Cor 3:18, AMPC)

Paul writes as one who is only too-aware of his human weakness:

> I do not understand my own actions. For I do not do what I want, but I do the very thing I hate... For I know that nothing good dwells within me, that is, in my flesh. I can will what is right, but I cannot do it. For I do not do the good I want, but the evil I do not want is what I do. Now if I do what I do not want, it is no longer I that do it, but sin that dwells within me...Wretched man that I am! Who will rescue me from this body of death? (Rom 7:15–24)

He discovers the Answer to his question!

HUMANITY TRANSFORMED

In this chapter we see how the Transfiguration enables frail humanity to meet empowering divinity, human fatigue comes face-to-face with the energies of God!

The Orthodox liturgical texts for the feast celebrate the revelation in Christ of "the nature of man"—and humanity's potentiality in Christ:

> He was transfigured before them,
> manifesting the loveliness of the original beauty...
> In His own person He showed them the nature of humanity
> arrayed in the original beauty of the Image.[3]

> O Christ with invisible hands You fashioned humanity in Your image
> now You have displayed the original beauty in this same human body
> revealing it, not as in an image, but as You are in Your own self
> according to Your essence, being both God and man.[4]

> Now the invisible has become visible to the apostles:
> On Mount Tabor the Godhead has shone forth before them in the flesh...
> Struck with wonder, on Mount Tabor the apostles trembled with fear
> before the beauty of the divine Kingdom.

> For You went up to this mountain with Your Disciples
> and were transfigured, O Christ,
> making the image that had grown dark in Adam
> to shine once again like lightning,
> and transforming it into the glory and splendor of Your own Divinity.[5]

---

3. *Festal Menaion*, 476.
4. *Festal Menaion*, 487.
5. Orthodox Church in America.

Kallistos Ware puts it plainly:

> The glory which shone from Jesus on Tabor is a glory that all mankind is called to share. On Mount Tabor we see Christ's human nature—the human substance which He took from us—filled with splendor, "made godlike" or "deified." What has happened to human nature in Christ can happen also to the humanity of Christ's followers. The Transfiguration, then, reveals to us the full potentiality of our human nature: it shows us the glory which our humanity once possessed and the glory, which by divine grace, it will recover on the Last Day.[6]

Human Transfiguration and Deification

Gregory Palamas (1296–1359), though he lived on another holy mountain—Mount Athos in Greece—long pondered the transformative meaning of the event of Mount Tabor. The light of Tabor infiltrated and illuminated every aspect of his writing. In the fourteenth century the Eastern Church affirmed the validity of Palamas' teaching, but for the past six hundred years his perspectives have been almost forgotten, rediscovered only in the mid-20th century, through the scholarly work of pioneers such as Dumitru Stăniloae, John Meyendorff and others.[7] For Gregory, the key to discovering the transfiguring power of God in our own lives is actually participating in God's life.

He puts it: "In prayer...we are called to *participation* in divine life: this participation is also the true knowledge of God."[8] In his controversy with the Calabrian philosopher Barlaam, Palamas is insistent: "But hesychasts [those who practice stillness] know that the purified and illuminated mind, when clearly participating in the grace of God, also beholds other mystical and supernatural visions..."[9] His opponent Barlaam had denied such possibility, maintaining that God was unknowable and cannot be experienced in this life. But Gregory crafts an important distinction, already found in the Cappadocian Fathers like Gregory of Nyssa and Basil, between the utter transcendence of God—his essence—and the way God touches and transforms human lives—his uncreated energies. His essence will forever

---

6. *Festal Menaion*, 62.
7. Staniloae, *Experience of God*; Meyendorff, *St Gregory Palamas*.
8. Meyendorff, *Byzantine Theology*, 77.
9. Palamas, *Triads*, 58.

be beyond us, but if we are open, we can experience for ourselves, as did the apostles on Tabor, the very energies of God enlivening us and fueling us.

For Gregory this enables the divinization of humanity, permeated and renewed by the divine energies. The Transfiguration event was

> opening the eyes of the disciples and bringing them from blindness to sight. . .They were transformed, and only in this way did they see the transformation taking place amidst the very assumption of our perishability, with the deification through union with the Word of God in place of this. . . Let us strive to be illumined by this Light ourselves and encourage in ourselves love and striving towards the Unfading Glory and Beauty. Let us be set free by the illumination and knowledge of the incorporeal and ever-existing Light of our Savior transfigured on Tabor, in His Glory, and of His Father from all eternity, and His Life-Creating Spirit, Whom are One Radiance, One Godhead, and Glory, and Kingdom, and Power now and ever and unto ages of ages. Amen.[10]

This is an echo of Athanasius' dictum: "God became human that humans might become God." Men and women can become godlike, sharing in divine attributes: "he has granted to us his precious and very great promises, that through these you may escape from the corruption that is in the world because of passion, and become partakers of the divine nature" (2 Peter 1:4, RSV). This is an awesome view of the very purpose of human life, our fundamental vocation and destiny. A human life is invited to be a transformative journey as one becomes permeated and infused by the divine energies and we progress towards ever closer union with God and identification with God.

A Divine Alchemy

The experience of divinization or deification is a gradual process of an ennobling transformation of our human nature, a fulfillment and completion of the promises of our baptism. Within the crucible of God's longing for us, the human dross is transformed into divine love, by the flame of the Holy Spirit.

Maximos the Confessor (579–662)—much admired by Gregory—had written of the conversion of the "intellect", which denotes not clever

---

10. Palamas, "Sermon on Feast of Transfiguration." For another translation Daley, *Light on the Mountain*.

or academic thought, as we might read it, but rather a receptive and longing heart:[11]

> When the intellect (*nous*) practices contemplation, it advances in spiritual knowledge...the intellect is granted the grace of theology when, carried on wings of love...it is taken up into God and with the help of the Holy Spirit discerns—as far as this is possible for the human intellect—the qualities of God.[12]

Such knowledge is transforming:

> The intellect joined to God for long periods through prayer and love becomes wise, good, powerful, compassionate, merciful and long-suffering; in short, it includes with itself almost all the divine qualities.

This echoes St Paul's conviction: "the fruit of the Spirit is love, joy, peace, patience, kindness, generosity, faithfulness, gentleness, and self-control" (Gal 5:22–23). Maximos testifies to a process whereby, within a synergy or working together with God, our human fiery energies and desires ("incensiveness") become changed, bit by bit, into love for God. For Maximos, we must allow God, working in partnership with our will and decisiveness, to so redirect our self-indulgent passions towards him, that we progressively become more like him, ourselves embracing the divine qualities:

> The one who combines the practice of the virtues with spiritual knowledge is a person of power. Practicing the virtues withers our desire and tames our incensiveness. By spiritual knowledge we give wings to our intellect [understanding divine truth through immediate experience, intuition] and go out of ourselves to God. When one's intellect is constantly with God, desire grows beyond all measure into an intense longing for God and one's incensiveness is completely transformed into divine love. For by continual participation in the divine radiance the intellect becomes totally filled with light...filling us with an incomprehensible and intense longing for Him and with unceasing love, thus drawing us entirely away from worldly things to the Divine.[13]

---

11. Defined as "The highest facility in humanity, through which one knows God by means of direct apprehension or spiritual perception. The intellect does not function by abstract concepts or deductive reasoning, but understands divine truth by immediate experience, intuition in the depths of the soul; it constitutes the innermost aspect of the heart." Palmer et al, *Philokalia*, Vol 1, 262.

12. Maximos the Confessor, "Four Hundred Texts on Love", *Philokalia*, Vol 2, 69.

13. *Philokalia*, Vol 2, 74.

TABOR TODAY!

In Gregory's view, deification is a return to humanity's original condition. Created in the image of God, humans actualize the likeness through union with God. The fall of Adam meant his separation from beauty and light but in Christ we regain the lost beauty of holiness after the image of God. The vision of the divine light is a return to the innocent state of humanity: in paradise, Adam was clothed with a garment of light, which he lost through sin; on Tabor, Christ clothes the disciples with this shining garment.

Gregory believes that the experience and promise of Mount Tabor does not belong only to past history or to a future hope of divine light in heaven. It is for today, for us to discover right now:

> The transformation of our human nature, its deification and transfiguration—were these not accomplished in Christ from the start, from the moment He assumed our nature? Thus He was divine before, but He bestowed at the time of His Transfiguration a divine power upon the eyes of the apostles and enabled them to look up and see for themselves. The light, then, was not an hallucination but will remain for eternity, and has existed from the beginning.
>
> But if Christ was such and will remain such for eternity, He is also still the same today. It would indeed be absurd to believe that such was His nature up to the most divine vision on Tabor, and that it will always be such in the Age to Come, but that it has become different in the intervening period, setting aside this glory. Today also He is seated in the same splendor, "at the right hand of the Majesty on high." All then must follow and obey Him Who says, "Come, let us ascend the holy and heavenly mountain, let us contemplate the immaterial divinity of the Father and the Spirit, which shines forth in the only Son."[14]

We realize that we are called to become Light-bearers. We celebrate our capacity to welcome the divine energies into every part of our life. Deification is the goal of human existence. At a time when human nature is seen in all its fragility, Gregory offers us the highest possible view of humanity. We may rejoice again in our potentiality: we are made in the image and likeness of God. As Lossky puts it: "I for my part believe that this is the only conception of the Image [of God in humanity] which can fulfil the demands of a Christian anthropology: Humanity created 'in the image' is the person

---

14. Palamas, *Triads*, 3:15,16.

capable of manifesting God in the extent to which his nature allows itself to be penetrated by deifying grace."[15]

Gregory celebrates our potentiality:

> We who participate in the divine energy...ourselves become, in a sense, Light; we are united to the Light and with the Light we see in full consciousness all that remains hidden for those who do not have this grace; we thus surpass not only the corporeal senses, but also all that can be known by the mind...for the pure in heart see God...who, being the Light, abides in us and reveals Himself to those who love Him, to His beloved ones.[16]

Here below, even in a land of shadow and deep darkness, we can radiate the divine light in our lives—this is why we are here. And we look forward to our eternal destiny, for "the righteous will shine like the sun in the kingdom of their Father" (Matt 13:43).

Anastasius of Sinai (7th century) sums up the wonder of our transfiguration in a powerful sermon he preached for its feast day at the monastery at the foot of Sinai, beneath the great mosaic of the Transfiguration:

> For today the Lord has truly appeared on the mountain; today, the old nature belonging to Adam—once made in the image of God, but dimmed to resemble the shapes of idols—is transformed in shape once again, transfigured to its ancient beauty in God's image and likeness. Today, on the mountain, an aimless, idolatrous nature has been altered, never to change again, and now sparkles with the shining brilliance of the divinity...
>
> Our hope is that, bathed in a vision of him, flooded with light, we might be changed for the better and joined together as one...With him, let us also flash like lightening before spiritual eyes, renewed in the shape of our souls and made divine, transformed with him in order to be like him, always being deified, always changing for the better...
>
> Let us run forward, boldly and brightly, then, let us enter into the cloud—this one becoming Moses, and that one Elijah, this one James and that one John! Be lifted up like Peter, to a vision, a mental image, of God; be changed by a good and holy transformation...
>
> What could be more blessed, more lofty, or more precious than this, to be with God and to be like God in form—to be in the

---

15. Lossky, *Image and Likeness*, 139.

16. Palamas, "Sermon for the Feast of the Presentation of the Blessed Virgin in the Temple", quoted by Lossky, *Image and Likeness*, 61.

light? So then, let each of us, who has received God in our heart, and who has been transfigured into that divine form, say in our joy: "It is good for us to be here, where everything is full of light, where there is joy and good spirits and exaltation, where everything in our hearts is peaceful and calm and free from conflict, where God is to be seen."[17]

Anastasius prays with joy: "You constantly form and transform our lack of form and shape for the better, by Your unchanging power of transformation!"[18]

"This is My Body—and Yours!"

In the Transfiguration the disciples are invited to gaze in wonderment at the body of Christ—physicality transformed. Particular mention or allusion is made to his face (Luke 9:29) and his hands ("he touched them", Matt 17:7). If the Transfiguration is saying something about our human divinization, it begins with the body. It is not an ethereal, ephemeral, esoteric dream or a vague, wafting apparition—but an almost-erotic embodiment, a way of sensing that is about enfleshment of the Divine within human corporeality. As Dorothy Lee observes: "Jesus' flesh is the place where the glory abides...In the Incarnation, the glory of God gleams through the flesh of Jesus...the flesh becomes the medium of glory."[19] There is an element of sensuality and of the sensory in the episode—the disciples seeing, hearing, being soaked by wet mist on their faces and touched by the outstretched hand of Jesus—and we will note later (ch.6) that the spiritual senses were activating new ways of perception. So far from being irrelevant or remote the Transfiguration has much to say about how we see our own bodies, and their potential.

It is crossing another divide, healing another dichotomy: spirituality meets physicality, body embraces soul, outer and inner identity are joined. The Transfiguration is the supreme inspiration for body positivity and reverence for our own physical temple. In respecting yourself you are honoring God your Creator. Holding up a mirror to us the Transfiguration declares: "Discover your own beauty in Christ. Live out your baptismal dignity as a child of God. Leave shame and poor body-image behind. Realize your potential to be radiant. Rejoice—your worth does not come from what

17. Daley, *Light on the Mountain*, 165, 168–69.
18. Daley, *Light on the Mountain*, 173.
19. Lee, *Transfiguration*, 126.

other people think of you—it comes from what God thinks of you and God declares you to be beautiful!" It might even have something to say about sexuality and sexual identity. . .

Significance Where Identity is Denigrated

If our own sense of identity—including sexual identity—is denied, or suppressed we can especially receive such a vision as Good News. Brian Flanagan observes:

> This idea of *theosis* or divinization is shocking language, and it's meant to be, because it's language that's trying to point to the new idea of the relation between God and creation that Jesus' Incarnation exemplifies. It's odd language. Queer language, even. In his book *That We Might Become God: The Queerness of Creedal Christianity* Andy Buechel draws upon the meanings of "queer" as strange, as LGBTQ, and as breaking apart easy identities and seemingly fixed boundaries to unpack the ultimate boundary-breaking of God becoming human—and, by extension, the boundary-breaking of humans becoming divine through their participation in Christ.
>
> From this queer perspective, the story of Christianity is a story of a God who wants to be close to us, breaking through the categories of identity in which we have sought comfort and convenience. What could be more queer, Buechel suggests, than the idea of God become human? Or the idea of humanity and creation as a whole participating so intimately in the life of God?
>
> From this angle, the Transfiguration is not only a story about Jesus revealing something about himself to his friends, but it's also a story about Jesus revealing something about us, and about who we are called to be: to remind us of what we are capable of, and what our God is hoping of each of us to become as we are graced into being children of God. If we hold on to that possibility, then this is not only a story about Jesus' past, but also a story about our—about *your*—future. God calls everyone to the always more beyond our limits. . .[20]

---

20. Flanagan, "Jesus' Transfiguration".

INTO AN UNKNOWN WORLD

I experienced the process of grace transforming nature and humanity inching towards its potential in a quite unexpected way—on top of Mount Tabor itself, when I was there for a few days' retreat in 2010 and welcomed warmly by a bunch of men in their 20s and 30s. For some years a community of young men served the pilgrims and guests, cooking, gardening, assisting in a multitude of ways with the Franciscan guesthouse. I found out that they were members of a movement called MONDO X. When I asked one of the men what this meant, he said: "We are being invited into an unknown world. We do not know what to expect, but we know it will be different, better than our previous lives. X conveys the idea that we cannot predict what God will do in us on Tabor. But it will be healing and empowering." As they learn new skills in hospitality and agriculture, they discover liberation from the captivity of drug and alcohol abuse, for they are all ex-addicts recovering their sense of dignity, hoping to also offer local young people who are victims of drugs a path to liberation.

I discovered that MONDO X had been founded by Franciscan Father Eligio Gelmini for the rehabilitation of drug and alcohol addicts. "X is the unknown in every person's life," says Father Eligio. "It means helping people to let go of appearances and lead them to look into their heart, because the true face of a person is the mystery of the heart." Riccardo Liguori explains: "Young people can find themselves and reconcile themselves with life by having an experience that leads them to live in communion and in a very welcoming environment where they can pray, meditate and work."[21]

Let's meet Bruno, Adriano and Michele among the ten residents helping the small Franciscan community to welcome pilgrims in the sanctuary of the Transfiguration of Jesus...

> After leaving the kitchen, Bruno goes to the garden. Below Mount Tabor lie the hills of Galilee. The gardener breathes deeply and begins to work: "The time I spend here is one of the most peaceful of my life." Bruno is one of the young people addicted to drugs or alcohol who currently lives in the homes of the MONDO X community, looking for ways to escape from that slavery.
>
> After eight years of community life in Italy, Adriano was entrusted with the responsibility of the new house on Tabor two years ago. "We encourage each other to learn love for our brothers, respect and also to sacrifice ourselves." In Adriano's experience,

---

21. Liguori, "Father Eligio".

the rigidity of the rules is healthy: most young people come from a total absence of rules and find here a framework with which to put their lives in order. The religious aspect in MONDO X, he emphasizes, is an invitation, not an obligation. However, he is convinced that "the voice that calls in the heart of man" is God himself, and prayer is the only true source of energy.

This is also true for Michele, who will be Adriano's successor. He considers himself "born, dead and resurrected": drugs, he says, first of all kill a person spiritually, and having rediscovered this dimension is the greatest treasure for them.

The path that leads to inner freedom passes through the smallness of everyday life. The Tabor group always has a lot to do: every day thousands of pilgrims visit the sanctuary. While the four Franciscan friars on the holy mountain take care of the church and pastoral care, the members of MONDO X rediscover themselves, their human vocation and identity and dignity.[22]

Atop the Mount of Transfiguration itself, the vulnerable but determined men of MONDO X show us something about the way divine grace can unlock yet-untapped human potential. They remind us of the human capacity for transformation. They experience life atop Tabor as affirming, empowering and healing. That is very much part of the message of the mountain of Transfiguration!

REDISCOVERING OUR TRUE IDENTITY

The Transfiguration has, we noted, important echoes of the Baptism of Christ. The Father's voice is heard from heaven, making similar affirmations:

> "You are my Son, the Beloved; with you I am well pleased." (Mark 1:11)

> "This is my Son, the Beloved." (Mark 9:7)

Both events involve the Holy Trinity: in the baptism in Jordan the Spirit's presence is represented in a dove; here in the enveloping cloud. As we have seen already, both are set in the midst of creation: the River points to the Mountain. Significantly, both speak to the question of our human dignity.

The Transfiguration evokes our own baptism. In the Transfiguration event the disciples get wet! They are saturated by the water of the cloud, the palpable wet fog. The Greek word for *baptize* means not only to immerse:

22. Fröhlich, "MONDO X al Tabor".

the word is used also to denote "plunge, sink, drench, overwhelm." Truly, the Transfiguration was an immersive experience in more than one sense!

Transfiguration is a Mirror

We're seeing that the Transfiguration is not only a window into heaven—it also holds up a mirror to our human dignity and destiny: "See what love the Father has given us, that we should be called children of God; and that is what we are" (1 John 3:1, JB). We glimpse ourselves in Jesus. We too hear the Father's baptismal affirmation speaking to our souls: "You are my Beloved, I am very pleased with you!" As in the waters of Baptism we discover our true calling and our very identity—to be a cherished child of God—so in the wet mists of the Transfiguration we see not only the glory we may one day share, but the very light in which we are invited to dwell daily. We see our true dignity in the person of Jesus, our nobility of soul and body.

Son of Man

This is emphasized by the way in which the Transfiguration in Mark is bracketed and held within a Son of Man Christology. Both before and after, there are two clear references to Jesus as the Son of Man, suggesting in this event we should view Jesus through the lens of the Son of Man:

> He then began to teach them that the Son of Man must suffer many things. (8:31)

> If anyone is ashamed of me and my words in this adulterous and sinful generation, the Son of Man will be ashamed of them when he comes in his Father's glory with the holy angels. (8:38)

> As they were coming down the mountain, he ordered them to tell no one about what they had seen, until after the Son of Man had risen from the dead. (9:9)

> How then is it written about the Son of Man, that he is to go through many sufferings... (9:12)

Elusive and enigmatic—that is what recent research concludes about the meaning of the phrase "Son of Man."[23] Attention had formerly been given

---

23. See Burkett, *Son of Man Debate*; Müller, *The Expression "Son of Man"*; Hurtado & Owen. "*Who is This Son of Man?*"; Barr, *Jesus Remembered*, 724–25; Dunn & McKnight,

to its possible significance as an apocalyptic title (see Dan 7:13; John 5:27). With or without capitalization, it was once widely believed that the phrase had strong messianic intentions, but this view was strongly challenged in the last century following analysis of the wider range of literature now available from the period, such as the Dead Sea scrolls and the Nag Hammadi library. But it points, intriguingly, to a fresh understanding of Jesus: universal brother.

Today, scholars favor reading it as a designation of essential humanity, its most obvious meaning. The Hebrew *ben adam* denotes "son of Adam"—child of mankind. The Aramaic phrase *bar enash* means "human being" or "the human one". The NRSV often translates "son of man" as "mortal." The striking thing about the New Testament, in contrast with the Hebrew Scriptures, is that the words "son of man" are used with the definite article "The" (*ho huios tou anthropou* in Greek). It has become a sort of title for Jesus, that could almost be translated "child of humanity", "child of the universe"—or, as we used to say, "Everyman." This underlines for us the idea that what we see in Jesus, we may become. He represents humanity in its completion, fulfilment. He holds up a mirror to us—showing us a glimpse of our own destiny and calling. He stands on Tabor in our name, as our exemplar. We gaze at him in his glory and see ourselves. He is the Human One.[24] He is us.

Son of God

Yet within the Transfiguration event itself Jesus is presented as Son of God, as the Father's voice is heard from the cloud: "This is my Son, the Beloved." As in the opening line of Mark's gospel and at the baptism, the Son of God Christology emphasizes Jesus' filial relationship with his Father. John of Damascus (675—749) celebrates how humanity and divinity meet in the person of Jesus:

> It was by the Father's good pleasure that his only begotten Son and Word became incarnate, which brought about the union of the whole universe in his only begotten Son. For humanity is a microcosm linking in itself all visible and invisible being, sharing as it does in the nature of both, and so it must surely have pleased the Lord, the creator and ruler of the universe, for divinity and humanity and thus all creation to be united in his only

Historical Jesus.

24. Favored translation of Son of Man in the Common English Bible.

begotten and consubstantial Son, so that God might be all in all. God declares: "This is my Son, the radiance of my glory, who bears the stamp of my own nature, through whom I created the angels, through whom the vault of heaven was made firm and the earth established. He upholds the universe by his powerful word and by the life-giving and guiding Spirit which proceeds from his mouth. As a man he is sent, but as God he abides in me and I in him. Listen to him, for he has the words of eternal life."[25]

"Look to Him, and Be radiant; Your Faces Shall Never Know Shame" (Ps 34:5)

In the Transfiguration, we glimpse our sublime destiny and potential, our capacity for divinization, deification, here below. The Roman Collect puts it well:

> *God our Father,*
> *in the transfigured glory of Christ your Son,*
> *you strengthen our faith*
> *by confirming the witness of your prophets,*
> *and show us the splendor of your beloved sons and daughters.*
> *As we listen to the voice of your Son*
> *help us to become heirs to eternal life with him*
> *who lives and reigns with you and the Holy Spirit,*
> *one God for ever and ever, Amen.*

Dare we enter the divine light—even participate in the energies of God—if it might alter us, reshape us, make us different?

To live a transfigured life is to be aware of our mortality—and thus be gentle with ourselves—and at the same time to rejoice in our God-given dignity, to celebrate our true identity in Christ and to flourish in our divine potentiality. The Transfiguration urges us to give up on self-pity or low self-esteem and catch a glimpse of our beauty in Christ. The human and the Divine meet in the paradox well-expressed by Paul:

> He said to me, "My grace is sufficient for you, for power is made perfect in weakness." So, I will boast all the more gladly of my weaknesses, so that the power of Christ may dwell in me. Therefore I am content with weaknesses, insults, hardships, persecutions, and

---

25. John of Damascus, "Homily on the Transfiguration", *PG* 96, 572–73.

calamities for the sake of Christ; for whenever I am weak, then I am strong. (2 Cor 12:9–10)

As Henri Le Saux puts it succinctly:

> The whole mystery of the Transfiguration is a vivid symbol of our deification through our entry into Christ's glory.[26]

QUESTIONS FOR REFLECTION

1. What erodes self-worth today and causes people to forever compare themselves with others?

2. "Therefore lift your drooping hands and strengthen your weak knees, and make straight paths for your feet, so that what is lame may not be put out of joint, but rather be healed" (Heb 12:12,13). How can we encourage people recover a wholesome self-image, that we all may be "growing into maturity with a stature measured by Christ's fullness" (Eph 4:13, CSB)?

3. How do you find yourself responding to the stunning language of human deification or divinization?

4. "The most courageous thing we will ever do is to bear humbly the mystery of our own reality."[27] What do you make of this?

5. How do you find yourself responding to Macrina Wiederkehr's prayer, "God, help me to believe the truth about myself, no matter how beautiful it may be"?[28] Respond with both your head and your heart!

PRAYER EXERCISE

If possible, sit in the sun or in a light place.

Allow yourself to bathe in the light of Christ. Receive his healing light into the center of your soul. May this be a restorative, empowering time with Jesus. Permit his rays to penetrate the hidden recesses of your heart, dispelling and driving away all lingering negative thoughts: permit yourself

---

26. Abhishiktananda, *Saccidananda*, 102.
27. Rohr, *Everything Belongs*, 97.
28. Wiederkehr, *Seasons of Your Heart*.

to delight in your God-given beauty and promise yourself that you will never underestimate yourself again!

Symeon the New Theologian (949–1022) will help us. Based in Constantinople, for 25 years he was abbot of St Mamas monastery. Called in the east "the greatest mystic of the Middle Ages", his central conviction was that the Holy Spirit makes possible a conscious encounter with Christ and, in some sense, the vision of God in this life.

> What else is so dear to God and welcome as a contrite and humble heart, and pride laid low in a spirit of humility? It is in such a condition of soul that God Himself comes to dwell and make His rest.
>
> "Have mercy on me, Son of David, and open the eyes of my soul, so that I may see the light of the world, even You, Who are God, and may become even I, a child of the day. . .O Merciful One, send the Comforter even to me, so that He may teach me the things concerning You; and O God of all, declare what is Yours to me. Illumine me with the true light, O Compassionate One, so that I may see the glory which You had with Your Father before the world was made. Abide even in me, as You have said, so that I, too, may become worthy of abiding in You, and may then consciously enter into You and consciously possess You within myself. . ."[29]

In *Hymns of Divine Love* (also called *Hymns of Divine Eros*), Symeon describes his vision of God as uncreated divine light, an experience of divine luminosity. Using his words, pray that such an experience will be yours, too:

> But, Oh, what intoxication of light, Oh, what movements of fire!
> Oh, what swirlings of the flame in me, miserable one that I am,
> coming from You and Your glory!
> The glory I know it and I say it is your Holy Spirit,
> who has the same nature with You, and the same honor, O Word;
> O God of the universe!
> I fall down in adoration before You.
> I thank You that You have made me worthy to know, however little it may be,
> the power of Your divinity.[30]

---

29. Symeon, *On the Mystical Life*, Vol 2.
30. Symeon, *Discourses*. Hymn 25.

Struggle for control: Arch of Crusader Fortress atop Tabor

3

Daring
Between Control and Risk

MOST PEOPLE WANT AUTONOMY over their lives—to be in charge of decision-making, and of their use of time and resources. This leads sometimes to a manipulative spirit and even to "gaslighting." This applies to the life of prayer—we like to organize ourselves, and keep a firm grip on things so that nothing gets "out of control"—that is to say, out of our control. So in prayer the default position for many is discursive prayer, the prayer of words that we offer, not entering the risky land of silence. For many people prayer becomes dominated by intercession—which sounds compassionate—but might end up advising the Almighty on what do to next, according to our own perceptions and priorities—rather than surrendering to God our desires and longings, for ourselves and others, unconditionally, and putting ourselves at God's disposal. We find ourselves caught in a paradox between a natural need to remain in charge of our lives—indeed, taking responsibility—and a dawning sense that actually God is calling us to live in a state of joyful vulnerability, with reckless faith and deep trust—that we are being summoned to live in a state of utter openness to the Divine, and to God's surprises!

PETER'S STRUGGLE TO BE IN CONTROL

All three accounts record Peter's reaction to the Transfiguration event: "Rabbi, it is good for us to be here; let us make three dwellings, one for you, one for Moses, and one for Elijah." The evangelist adds the comment: "He did not know what to say, for they were terrified" (Mark 9:5,6).

What were Peter's motives in his plan to build three tents or tabernacles? Often in time of fear or stress one's true nature comes out. It seems that Peter wanted to regain mastery over a situation that was unfolding without his scheming. He had lost the initiative. He needed to take charge. Perhaps, also, he needed to box in the mystery of the appearances that was too great for his mind to grasp—he needed to get a handle on things, as we say. He needed to be able to take a grip on the situation, so he suggested that he would construct shelters to hold things in. Peter's heart quakes with fear of the unknown. But above all, he simply needed to be in control!

This image of Peter needing to be in control resonates with other episodes where this side of his character emerges. At the Sea of Galilee, Peter the fisherman could not accept, without arguing, Jesus' direction to put out into deep uncertain waters. "We have toiled all night. . .!" he protests (Luke 5:5). Peter liked to be in charge—he did not want to leave his place of security, and risk losing face. At Caesarea Philippi he took Jesus aside and remonstrated with him when he could not accept an idea of a suffering Son of Man which went well beyond his own narrow grasp of Jesus as Messiah (Mark 8:32). At the Last Supper (John 13), he at first refused to be washed by Jesus—he wanted things on his own terms. "You will never wash my feet!" On the night of the passion, he again manifested his stubborn desire to stay in control by keeping his distance from Jesus (Luke 22). His reaction on Tabor is "in character"! It is as if he wants to manipulate the situation for his own ends.

God's Response to his Request

It comes in the form of a dense mist or fog that envelops and enshrouds them: "Then a cloud overshadowed them . . . they entered the cloud" (Luke 9:34). The divine mystery was too big for any kind of tent! This can represent our own attempts in prayer to encase the untamable Divine with words, concepts and images. But precisely at the very point when Peter suggests the building of booths "while he was saying this a cloud came and overshadowed them; and they were afraid as they entered the cloud" (Luke 9:34). The response to human tent-building is a divine smothering or drenching in mysterious wet mist where visibility is reduced to nil. The cloud now dampens the senses and exuberant conceptualizing and silences the over-active mind. The cloud eclipses the sun: there has been, as it were, a change in the weather, from bright sunlight to darkening cloud, gloom and impenetrable haze. A swirling fog blankets the disciples.

This expresses well the sense of disorientation and confusion that one experiences in a baffling liminal place. In the cloud one feels out of control, not knowing which way to turn. It turns out to be a poignant symbol of that transition in prayer from active, discursive thinking to simpler loving. That also means a shift from predictable prayer to that which is more risky: from prescriptive prayer to something that is unpredictable. As Rowan Williams puts it: "We have to live in a world with all its risks. We must be prepared to be mentally and spiritually flung backwards, baffled in finding adequate words for this, even fearful at the prospect of discipleship it puts before us."[1]

On the Mount of Transfiguration the Divine is encountered in both light and cloud. The light represents the *kataphatic* tradition of prayer—where affirmations and declarations about God are made confidently: Jesus is light; "his face shone like the sun"; "his garments became white as light." But the cloud represents the *apophatic* tradition, where words give way to silence, where concepts about God dissolve into speechless wonder, where the unifying dense wet fog of the cloud enshrouds the disciples, blankets their fluttering minds and silences all attempts at talking.

MOSES' EXPERIENCE

This reference to the overshadowing cloud evokes the theophany on Mount Sinai, where God appears in "a thick cloud on the mountain". The Book of Exodus gives us an awesome and mysterious narrative:

> On the morning of the third day there was thunder and lightning, as well as a thick cloud on the mountain, and a blast of a trumpet so loud that all the people who were in the camp trembled. Moses brought the people out of the camp to meet God. They took their stand at the foot of the mountain. Now Mount Sinai was wrapped in smoke, because the Lord had descended upon it in fire; the smoke went up like the smoke of a kiln, while the whole mountain shook violently. As the blast of the trumpet grew louder and louder, Moses would speak and God would answer him in thunder. When the Lord descended upon Mount Sinai, to the top of the

---

1. Williams, *Dwelling of the Light*. The reference is to Theophan's icon of the Transfiguration.

> mountain, the Lord summoned Moses to the top of the mountain, and Moses went up. (Exod 19:16–20)
>
> When all the people witnessed the thunder and lightning, the sound of the trumpet, and the mountain smoking, they were afraid and trembled and stood at a distance, and said to Moses, "You speak to us, and we will listen; but do not let God speak to us, or we will die." Moses said to the people, "Do not be afraid; for God has come only to test you and to put the fear of him upon you so that you do not sin." Then the people stood at a distance, while Moses drew near to the thick darkness where God was. (Exod 20:18–21)
>
> Then Moses went up on the mountain, and the cloud covered the mountain. The glory of the Lord settled on Mount Sinai, and the cloud covered it for six days; on the seventh day he called to Moses out of the cloud. Now the appearance of the glory of the Lord was like a devouring fire on the top of the mountain in the sight of the people of Israel. Moses entered the cloud, and went up on the mountain. Moses was on the mountain for forty days and forty nights. (Exod 24:15–18)

The awesome theophany on Mount Sinai is paradoxical. There is dazzling light, fire and lightening; there is dense shrouding darkness and impenetrable cloud. We find God in light as he illumines our lives and makes us radiant with a sense of his presence. But we also encounter God in deep darkness—we cannot make anything out—we encounter the unknowable mystery of a God beyond the categories and concepts of human language. In Christian spirituality both approaches have their place—the *via positiva*, delighting in vivid metaphors and images faces the *via negativa*, which tells us that we need to go beyond images—they are only a starting point.

Moses Himself Reveals the Paradox

Moses face shone radiantly because he had encountered God in the shining brightness of his glory. He also met with God in the deep darkness. Moses' dilemma reflects the two approaches we have seen. What will Moses do? Will he come down from the mountain, among his people, with unveiled face to show the Israelites that he had seen God's glory and indeed experienced divine illumination? Or would he veil his face to conceal the glory so that the Israelites would know nothing of the mystery of the encounter?

Would Moses reveal or conceal? Would there be disclosure or hiddenness? This is what we wonder when we ascend the mount of prayer, and we will explore it further in the next chapter. For the moment, we name the paradox: will we find God in startling discoveries, insights, revelations? Or will we experience mystery, clouds of unknowing, that we cannot articulate to others, a God beyond human words? Maybe we will like Moses choose both ways—keeping our veil on and remaining silent about our unspeakable encounter with God, and also removing the veil so that we can share, somehow, the truths we have discovered about God.

Paul for his part, was also ambivalent. He tells us to have unveiled faces: "all of us, with unveiled faces, seeing the glory of the Lord as though reflected in a mirror, are being transformed into the same image from one degree of glory to another; for this comes from the Lord, the Spirit" (2 Cor 3:18). But in other places he will be more circumspect: "O the depth of the riches and wisdom and knowledge of God! How unsearchable are his judgments and how inscrutable his ways!" (Rom 11:33).

Gregory of Nyssa (335–95) in his *Life of Moses* reflects on the Christian vocation as a pilgrimage and journey for which the Israelites' escape from Pharaoh, their passage through the Red Sea, and their encounter with God at Sinai suggest a pattern or archetype that can be reflected in our own experience. The spiritual journey begins with baptism, prefigured in the crossing of the Red Sea, liberating a person from the captivity not of Pharaoh but of sin. The Christian pilgrim's journey, like the trek through the wilderness, will be marked by God's provision (as in manna, water from the rock), God's guidance (the pillar of cloud), human failure and spiritual battles (represented in conflict with Amalekites). Ultimately all this leads to the ascent of the mountain of divine knowledge, represented in Sinai. Gregory claims that an integral element in the Christian pilgrimage is the encounter with divine darkness, as it was for Moses:

> What does it mean that Moses entered the darkness and then saw God in it? What is now recounted seems to be contradictory to the first theophany [the Burning Bush], for *then* the Divine was beheld in light but *now* he is seen in darkness. Let us not think that this is at variance with the sequence of things we have contemplated spiritually. Scripture teaches by this that religious knowledge comes at first to those who receive it as light. Therefore what is perceived to be contrary to religion is darkness, and the escape from darkness comes about when one participates in light.

> But as the mind progresses and, through an ever greater and more perfect diligence, comes to perceive reality, as it approaches more nearly to contemplation, it sees more clearly what of the divine nature is uncontemplated.

It is a sign, then, of spiritual maturity and evidence that one is making progress in the spiritual life if one comes to encounter God in the darkness. Gregory goes on:

> Leaving behind everything that is observed—not only what sense comprehends but also what the intelligence thinks it sees—the soul keeps on penetrating deeper until, by the intelligence's yearning for understanding, it gains access to the invisible and the incomprehensible, and there it sees God. This is the true knowledge of what is sought; this is the seeing that consists in not seeing, because that which is sought transcends all knowledge, being separated on all sides by incomprehensibility as by a kind of darkness. Wherefore John the sublime, who penetrated into the luminous darkness, says. "No one has ever seen God", thus asserting that knowledge of the divine essence is unattainable not only by men but also by every intelligent creature.
>
> When, therefore, Moses grew in knowledge, he declared that he had seen God in the darkness, that is, that he had then come to know that what is divine is beyond all knowledge and comprehension, for the text says, "Moses approached the dark cloud where God was." What God? He who "made darkness his hiding place," as David says, who also was initiated into the mysteries in the same inner sanctuary.[2]

Gregory of Nyssa was the first writer to develop this message through the image of darkness; it was to become an important strand in thinking of spiritual development throughout the history of Christian spirituality. Danielou puts it: "In Gregory of Nyssa . . . the term 'darkness' takes on a new meaning and an essentially mystical connotation . . . Gregory's originality consists in the fact that he was the first to express this characteristic of the highest stages of mystical experience."[3]

In Moses' first encounter with God, in the Burning Bush, God appears as light, as illumination. For Gregory, this represents the beginning of the Christian conversion, a turning from the darkness of falsehood to the light

---

2. Gregory of Nyssa, *Life of Moses*, 95.
3. Danielou, "Introduction" in Musurillo, *From Glory to Glory,* 27.

of Christ. This process of illumination, for beginners, involves a purification of the soul from foreign elements.

However, as the Christian, like Moses, progresses along the spiritual journey, he or she is led into darkness: not a negative darkness but a "luminous darkness." This represents the unknowability of God: this is the apophatic spiritual path, which falls silent before the unspeakable mystery of God. Danielou puts it:

> After learning all that can be known of God, the soul discovers the limits of this knowledge; and this discovery is an advance, because now there is an awareness of the divine transcendence and incomprehensibility. We have then arrived at a negative, "apophatic" theology. For we have now an authentic experience, a true vision. And the darkness is a positive reality that helps us to know God—that is why it is called luminous. For it implies an awareness of God that transcends all determination, and thus it is far truer than any determined categorical knowledge. For here in this obscurity the soul experiences the transcendence of the divine nature, that infinite distance by which God surpasses all creation.[4]

For Gregory, the encounter with God in the dark is not a rarefied experience or only limited to Moses. He writes of his own brother Basil:

> Often we saw him enter the darkness where God was. By the mystical guidance of the Spirit he understood what was invisible to others, so that he seemed to be enveloped in that darkness in which the Word of God is concealed.[5]

Gregory tells us that in prayer we need to let go of our controlling tendencies, which are expressed in our fixation with finding the right words for God, the right boxes to put him in. We need sometimes to silence our words and still our best efforts at achieving successful or satisfying prayer and rather expose ourselves to the unknowability of God: to let God be God, in all his transcendent and unspeakable mystery. The apophatic approach of prayer learns to "let go and let God."

---

4. Danielou, "Introduction" in Musurillo, *From Glory*, 30. Gregory sees in the Song of Songs divine darkness both in unknowing and in the desire and yearning of the bride.

5. Gregory of Nyssa, *On His Brother Basil*, PG46.812C.

"Leave Behind You Everything Perceived and Understood"

In the fifth century, the writer known as **Dionysius** develops the thought of Gregory:

> Trinity!! Higher than any being,
>   any divinity, any goodness!
> Guide of Christians
>   in the wisdom of heaven!
> Lead us up beyond unknowing and light,
>   up to the farthest, highest peak
>   of mystic scripture,
>   where the mysteries of God's Word
>   lie simple, absolute and unchangeable
>   in the brilliant darkness of a hidden silence.
> Amid the deepest shadow
>   they pour overwhelming light
>   on what is most manifest.
> Amid the wholly unsensed and unseen
>   they completely fill our sightless minds
>   with treasures beyond all beauty.[6]

Dionysius echoes the thought of Gregory of Nyssa; indeed, he seems to have known his *Life of Moses*—he too uses a similar image to explore the significance of darkness. Thus he writes:

> Leave behind you everything perceived and understood, everything perceptible and understandable, all that is not and all that is, and, with your understanding laid aside, strive upward as much as you can toward union with him who is beyond all being and knowledge. By an undivided and absolute abandonment of yourself and everything, shedding all and freed from all, you will be uplifted to the ray of the divine shadow which is above everything that is.[7]

Within his Christianized Neo-Platonism, Dionysius finds the apex of the spiritual search.[8] Andrew Louth observes: "It is an experience beyond the

---

6. Pseudo-Dionysius, "Mystical Theology" *Complete Works*, 135. See Louth, *Denys the Aeropagite*.

7. Pseudo-Dionysius, "Mystical Theology" *Complete Works*, 135.

8. See perspective in McGinn, *Foundations of Mysticism*.

senses and beyond the intellect; it is a feeling awareness of a fragrance that delights and enraptures the soul."9

ENTER THE CLOUD OF UNKNOWING

The classic fourteenth century English text *The Cloud of Unknowing* invites us to experience the cloud of prayer. The author pursues a similar apophatic approach, cautious about the use of vivid images in relation to speaking of God, commending wordless silence rather than exuberant speech:

> When you first begin, you find only darkness and as it were a cloud of unknowing. You don't know what this means except that in your will you feel a simple steadfast intention reaching out towards God...Reconcile yourself to wait in this darkness as long as is necessary, but still go on longing after him whom you love. For if you are to feel him or to see him in this life, it must always be in this cloud, in this darkness.[10]

The *Cloud* pays attention to the affective aspects of prayer, rather than the cognitive aspects. It says of God: "He may well be loved, but not thought. By love he can be caught and held, but by thinking never."[11] The *Cloud* aids the identification of "signs" of spiritual progress or impediments to growth. It teaches that there are various signs, clues or evidences that suggest that the reader may be ready to make a transition in their praying from discursive, active thinking with words and images, as in meditations on the passion, towards the wordless silence and solitude of contemplation. One key indicator is that of desire or yearning: "our Lord in his great mercy has called you . . . leading you on to himself by your heart-felt desire."[12] The author wants to urge the Christian to step forward into a transfiguration-kind of prayer characterized by watching, waiting, longing . . . "So when you feel by the grace of God that he is calling you to this work, and you intend to respond, lift up your heart to God with humble love. . . It all depends on your desire."[13]

9. Louth, *Origins*, 91.

10. All quotations are from Wolters (tr.), *Cloud*, here 53,54. For a more recent translation see Walsh (tr.), *Cloud of Unknowing*.

11. Wolters, *Cloud*, 60.

12. Wolters, *Cloud*, 51. For the role of desire in spirituality see Sheldrake, *Befriending Our Desires*.

13. Wolters, *Cloud*, 61.

There are other clues or indicators that suggest that someone may be ready to enter more mystical, receptive prayer. One finds oneself unfulfilled by Peter's tents, representing prayer hemmed in by words. Even liturgical prayer or the daily office or traditional devotions come to feel constricting and stifling. The Cloud beckons.

LIGHT AND CLOUD TODAY

We glimpse other vital lessons in the transition from dazzling sunlight to darkening cloud. Jesus "went up the mountain to pray" and we've seen that Luke offers us this episode to teach us something about prayer. The first part of the Transfiguration story, the radiant light surrounding Christ, speaks to us of the times it is easy to pray: the light is shining. In bright times we can easily glimpse the glory and presence of God—in the beauty of creation, the playfulness of children, the smile of a friend or stranger. But we also face times when life is foggy, cloudy—when we can't see the way forward, when we find ourselves in a haze of confusion or indecision, or when the dark clouds of suffering, anxiety or illness hang overhead. We find ourselves in a cloud of struggle. The story of the Transfiguration assures us: God is in the light, but he is in the dark cloud too—indeed he speaks to us from the cloud, calling to us "Listen!" We are to discern his presence in the shadows, and try to hear what he is saying to us in them. Then we find ourselves, as Matthew puts it, in "a bright cloud" (Matt 17:5).

Experiencing Light and Dark Ourselves

In this changeable, unpredictable world, we stay positive by holding onto blessings and by celebrating the shafts of light that shine upon us. We're discovering fresh ways of appreciating creation, and coming to a renewed appreciation of others, understanding more deeply than ever before our human inter-connectedness and solidarity, and the fact that we really do need each other. We realize that we must never take things for granted: all is gift, not right. Daily, we have new opportunities to enjoy the gifts and graces of the Holy Spirit: maybe glimpsing new truths about compassion and self-sacrifice. Sometimes we witness courage and big-hearted responses to those in need. As the world shrinks, we increase our awareness of the poor and marginalized across the globe. Perhaps we have been learning how to convert unchosen loneliness into God-bearing solitude, isolation into spiritual retreat. We exult in the creativity shown by so many, not least the dedication and brilliance of scientists discovering new technologies. Such learnings are to be celebrated as light, as illumination of soul, even as enlightenment.

But from time-to-time we have also found ourselves plunged into many kinds of darkness. Some of these darknesses have been experienced as very negative times, including the darkness of fear, the gloom of bereavement, the shadows of despair. We have lingered in the darkness of unresolved issues, unanswered questions, uncertainty and even agnosticism—not knowing—unknowing. Sometimes we have been in a land of confusion and in a place of disorientation.

But maybe we can begin to see that God is in the darkness and in the questions. Gregory of Nyssa noted that Moses was in the thick darkness with God (Exod 20:21) and he re-assures us that it is actually OK to be in the dark, with God. God works in the dark. The darkness reminds us that God, sometimes revealing, is often infuriatingly, frustratingly incomprehensible, unknowable. It may feel as if he is present in times of light and absent in times of dark but actually he is waiting to be found in the dark. As Matthews cautions us, this summons us to a different mindset, and an expansion of our normal patterns of thought: "We have become used to thinking of the Christian faith in terms of the light that it provides, the illumination that it gives to the mind and soul. To understand it as a step into darkness requires a different frame of mind, a change of attitude for which we are little prepared."[14]

Yet this has been the challenge and opportunity of recent times. In hindsight, it may turn out to be life-transforming—the realization that in the dark we can watch and wait with God, that he is not faraway, he is close, even if unseen and unheard.

Learning with Peter

Peter must learn that to be a follower of Jesus is to be prepared to enter the place of risk, the place of Sinai-like danger, where there can be no controlling of a wild, unpredictable, untamable God. Mount Tabor is a place of exposure to the Divine, a place where Peter is invited to discover vulnerability, not the shielding safety of tents. Here he cannot hem himself in by self-protective tabernacles over which he holds the key. He must be

14. Matthews, *Both Alike to Thee*.

prepared to enter the disorientating cloud, which turns out to be the very place where God's voice will be heard (Luke 9:35).

To live the transfigured life is paradoxical indeed—to find life, we must lose it—we must release our grip on the tiller in order to guided divinely forward. We give up control, but we find everything. Vulnerability is not a condition to be avoided—it turns out to be the precondition of discovering God!

QUESTIONS FOR REFLECTION

1. What is needed to allow us to move from being in control to being in a place of vulnerability and openness before God? What steps do we need to take to be able to "let go, and let God"?

2. How far can you identify with Peter's experience? What lies behind the need to be in control?

3. Have you experienced any "Burning Bush" times or Mount Sinai times of enlightenment and illumination? Recall these moments and celebrate them.

4. Danielou writes: "The darkness is a positive reality that helps us to know God." Reflect on times of darkness in your life that actually led you to new insight or a deeper appreciation of truth.

5. How do you feel when you find yourself as it were in darkness and thick cloud, faced with the unknowability and incomprehensibility of God? How can we change bewilderment into wonderment?

PRAYER EXERCISE

This exercise is in two parts: in light and dark.

First, use your physical senses to awaken your spiritual senses. Take a prayer walk in creation. Look carefully at what you pass, and watch out for signs of the Divine, noticing what speaks to you of God. Look up and look down. Listen to the sounds with what Benedict called "the ears of your heart." Taste any fruit or dew, and "Taste and see that the Lord is good" (Ps 38:4). Enjoy the fragrances. Touch different surfaces and look for what Bonaventure called "the fingerprints of God." Let this be a sensual and sacramental experience, and way to stimulate the practice of your spiritual faculties.

Secondly, go to a quiet place and shut down your senses, closing your eyes. Feel the darkness and silence your active thinking. Breathe slowly and become aware of your breathing. Try to quieten your mind and listen. Give up controlling, organizing, striving. Become receptive to divine whispers. Rest in this "cloud" for as long as you can.

Mount Hermon from Lebanon

4

Shining
Between Revelation and Hiddenness

SHOULD WE WEAR OUR heart on our sleeve? Should we be enthusiastic or reticent about sharing our faith? To what extent is our faith not only personal but private? For what reasons might we hold back from speaking about our spirituality? We are often exhorted to be witnesses or evangelists—passing on to others what we have discovered for ourselves, bringing the Good News of Jesus to a needy world. But we find ourselves in a tension between such a Gospel imperative and the need to safeguard and protect what we have been entrusted with—while avoiding the danger of becoming buttoned-up or tight-lipped.

We have seen that the Transfiguration is, at once, a radiant epiphany and a mysterious concealment: dazzling light and enshrouding cloud. On the mountaintop, we encounter bright radiance and blanketing fog—secrets revealed and secrets concealed. We ponder further this paradox in this chapter.

Privatized Religion?

Sometimes spirituality gets a bad press. Attentiveness to our individual and personal spiritual journey can be regarded as self-indulgent, fostering a spirituality that is introverted, narcissistic, self-centered, closed in on itself, encouraging escapism, navel-gazing and insularity. Does spirituality provide a refuge from life's storms, a place of safety away from the harsh realities of life? Is it a distraction from, or evasion of, reality? Does it represent a flight from the world? A diversion to keep us peaceful, to insulate us and keep free from stress? Does the practice of prayer amount to luxuriating in self-absorption by spiritual pleasure-seekers? Does it encourage living in an ivory tower—or burying one's head in the sand? People's perceptions give fuel to this critique: spirituality is seen as a ghettoized, personal matter, a private concern, nurturing the inner world at the expense of the outer: it is about "me and Jesus." People sometimes talk of spirituality in terms of self-fulfillment or self-discovery, the exploration of the "spiritual side of themselves". It has been called "another bandwagon to jump on, or a market need to satisfy."[1] Pope Francis, calling us in his Apostolic Exhortation *Evangelii Gaudium* to radiate the joy of the Gospel and develop a missionary spirituality, observes:

> Today we are seeing in many pastoral workers . . . an inordinate concern for their personal freedom and relaxation . . . At the same time, the spiritual life comes to be identified with a few religious exercises which can offer a certain comfort but which do not encourage encounter with others, engagement with the world or a passion for evangelization. Mystical notions without a solid social and missionary outreach are of no help to evangelization . . . What is needed is the ability to cultivate an interior space which can give a Christian meaning to commitment and activity.[2]

The danger is that spirituality becomes seen as an esoteric and fringe activity, for those spiritual and heavenly-minded beings amongst us that perhaps have too much time on their hands! The focus becomes pandering to the ego and self-development. The all-pervasive individualism which infects so much of western society, allied to a consumerist approach to all things ("what can I get out of this, what's in this for me?"), can seep its way into how people approach spirituality. Spirituality can become a hobby, a recreational activity for self-entertainment. God becomes a private experience. In such light the Transfiguration event itself can be distorted into a spiritual entertainment, a sideshow, an irrelevance to contemporary concerns.

Postmodernist thinking has reinforced the divide between private and public, and considers spirituality, and indeed religion, as something that

---

1. Freeman, "Dangers of the Shallow End."
2. Pope Francis, *Evangelii Gaudium*, 46, 128.

pertains only to the subjective, private lives of individuals. Philip Sheldrake observes:

> If human solidarity is forgotten, contemplation becomes no more than spiritual self-delusion. A non-social experience, or one that is purely "spiritual" and removed from our material existence, is a self-centered concern for a false peace. The greatest danger for Christian spirituality is for it to become anti-material, spiritualized, and individualistic... There will be a tendency to retreat into prayer and "spiritual" experiences as ends in themselves without any obvious implications for our behavior and attitudes... Prayer that is unconcerned with the situation of our neighbor is pure self-indulgence.[3]

Eugene Peterson warns: "Every expression of spirituality, left to itself, tends towards being more about me and less about God."[4] Leech reminds us: "all spirituality must be judged by the vision of the coming age. The Kingdom is the standard by which Christian disciples live, and by that standard they discern the signs of the times."[5]

Yet, on the face of it, the event of the Transfiguration seems to encourage, even require, a strict separation from the world.

The Transfiguration is Framed within Secrecy: "Tell No One"

Prefacing the event at Caesarea Philippi is Jesus curing a blind man at Bethsaida, marking the theme of secrecy:

> They came to Bethsaida. Some people brought a blind man to him and begged him to touch him. He took the blind man by the hand and led him out of the village...; and when he had put saliva on his eyes and laid his hands on him, he asked him, "Can you see anything?" And the man looked up and said, "I can see people, but they look like trees, walking." Then Jesus laid his hands on his eyes again; and he looked intently and his sight was restored, and he saw everything clearly. Then he sent him away to his home, saying, "Do not even go into the village or tell anyone in the village." (Mark 8: 22–26)

---

3. Sheldrake, *Images of Holiness*, 92–94.
4. Peterson, *Christ Plays*, 47.
5. Leech, *Soul Friend*, 190.

The revelation of the Transfiguration is framed in the gospels by a repeated emphasis on secrecy. The accounts are, in fact, bookended or bracketed by a solemn prohibition:

> Jesus went on [from Bethsaida] with his disciples to the villages of Caesarea Philippi; and on the way he asked his disciples, "Who do people say that I am?"
> And he sternly ordered them not to tell anyone about him. (Mark 8:27–30)

Luke 9:21 is even more emphatic: "He sternly ordered and commanded them not to tell anyone."

After the event:

> As they were coming down the mountain, he ordered them to tell no one about what they had seen, until after the Son of Man had risen from the dead. So they kept the matter to themselves, questioning what this rising from the dead could mean. (Mark 9. 9–10)

It is a theme we encounter in the prophet Isaiah:

> Truly, you are a God who hides himself.

> Truly you are a God who lies hidden. (Isa 45:15)

> I will give you the treasures of darkness and riches hidden in secret places, so that you may know that it is I, the Lord, the God of Israel, who call you by your name. (Isa 45:3)

> You have heard; now see all this; and will you not declare it? From this time forward I make you hear new things, hidden things that you have not known. (Isa 48:6)

Jesus too will echo this paradox, appearing both as revealer and enigma, not least in the question of his possible identity as Messiah.

MESSIANIC HOPE

If we trace the development of messianic hope in the Hebrew Scriptures and inter-testamental period, we see how the theme of humanity's longing for a revealer occurs again and again. There is a thirst and desire for someone who will make plain, not only the truth about God, but also the truth about humanity:

> The people who walked in darkness have seen a great light . . .
> For a child has been born for us, a son given to us;
> and he is named Wonderful Counsellor . . . (Isa 9:2,4,6)

The same prophet depicts the coming Messiah as one who will reveal new insight into the nature of God:

> The spirit of the Lord shall rest on him,
> the spirit of wisdom and understanding,
> the spirit of counsel and might,
> the spirit of knowledge and the fear of the LORD. (Isa 11:1–3)

The Messiah is to be an anointed king-like figure who will unveil the mystery of God. The hope for a divinely-appointed king strengthened during two periods in particular. During the Exile (586- 516), when the Israelite population was displaced, the longings for a future deliverer/ revealer intensified. Jeremiah looked for a figure who would establish a new covenant (Jer 31). Ezekiel saw the longed-for savior in terms of a shepherd-king after the pattern of David (Ezek 34). Later, there was a rekindling of messianic hope when the Jewish people experienced the failure of the Hasmonean kings to uphold peace and justice (152–63 BC). The Essene community at Qumran, on the shore of the Dead Sea, expected two messiahs: a political liberator and a spiritual revealer.

The messianic hope finds its fulfilment in the pages of the New Testament. In the account of the annunciation, Gabriel says to Mary: "He will be great, and will be called the Son of the Most High, and the Lord God will give to him the throne of his ancestor David." Luke and Matthew locate the birth of Jesus in Bethlehem precisely to affirm that he is Messiah: according to prophecy, the Messiah has to be born in the City of David. The Pauline writings celebrate the revealing of the mystery: "he [God] has made known to us the mystery of his will, according to his good pleasure that he set forth in Christ, as a plan for the fullness of time, to gather up all things in him, things in heaven and things on earth" (Eph 1:9,10). Paul delights in what has happened: " 'What no eye has seen, nor ear heard, nor the human heart conceived, what God has prepared for those who love him'—these things God has revealed to us" (1 Cor 2:9).

MESSIANIC REVELATION

If we want to know what God is like, we take a long look at Jesus. We see him healing the sick and welcoming the marginalized, and we realize that this is our God, a God who excludes no one from his enveloping love. We see Jesus teaching and sharing words of deepest wisdom, and we realize afresh how God wants to guide and shape our lives. When we see Jesus stretching out his arms wide on the Cross, we glimpse the depths of God's love for us. When we discover the Risen Christ breaking out of the prison of death, we recognize that nothing can defeat or overpower the indestructible grace of God.

Unveiling the Secrets of the Kingdom

Yet when we examine the Synoptic gospels, we encounter the theme of mystery. Jesus says to the disciples: "To you has been given the secret of the kingdom of God" (Mark 4:11). The Greek word *musterion* denotes something as yet unknown: "secret, especially of religious matters known only to the initiated."[6] In Matthew's gospel the word is the plural *mysteria*: there are many secrets to be discovered (Matt 13:11). Jesus diverges hidden things and initiates his closest followers into knowledge of the Divine: he senses they are ready to receive this revelation. The English word "reveal" means literally "to remove the veil". As the veil separating humanity from the Divine, the heavy curtain before the Holy of Holies in the Temple sanctuary, is ripped apart from top to bottom at the time of the crucifixion, so throughout the ministry of Jesus there is an unveiling of the Divine. Jesus announces the imminent inbreaking of the reign of God.

In Luke's gospel we note how Jesus as Messiah reveals God's compassion and acceptance to those who are marginalized. In chapter 15 his parables proclaim the longing of God for people gone astray. Jesus celebrates *apokalupsis*, disclosure or revelation, taking place in the pastoral experience of the Seventy and in his own ministry:

> At that same hour Jesus rejoiced in the Holy Spirit and said, "I thank you, Father, Lord of heaven and earth, because you have hidden these things from the wise and the intelligent and have revealed them to infants; yes, Father, for such was your gracious will. All things have been handed over to me by my Father; and

---

6. Zerwick & Grosvenor, *Grammatical Analysis*, 111.

no one knows who the Son is except the Father, or who the Father is except the Son and anyone to whom the Son chooses to reveal him." (Luke 10:21,22)

Luke's gospel gives us glimpses into the hidden emotional life of Christ. Weeping over Jerusalem, Jesus lays bare the longing of his inmost heart (Luke 19:41–44, 13:34). In Gethsemane, Luke alone tells us, Jesus embraces an agony and struggle of mind and spirit (Luke 22:44).

When we turn to Mark's gospel, we encounter a Messiah who makes known God's longing in the calling of the disciples by the water's edge (1:16ff). He demonstrates the healing love of God as the whole city crowds around the house in Capernaum, seeking cure and relief (1:32f). In Mark's gospel, Jesus comes to declare the Kingdom with urgency: "'Let us go on to the neighboring towns, so that I may proclaim the message there also; for that is what I came out to do.' And he went throughout Galilee, proclaiming the message in their synagogues and casting out demons" (Mark 1:38, 39). He instructs the healed demoniac to go home to his friends and tell them what God has done: to open the mystery to others (5:19). This announcing of God's reign leads up to a pivotal moment in the gospel when Jesus asks: "who do you say I am?"

But in response to Peter's declaration "You are the Messiah", Jesus says something stunning and unexpected: "And he sternly *ordered* them not to tell anyone about him" (Mark 8:30). The Greek word has this force and effect: he rebukes Peter, takes him to task, and absolutely forbade him to speak of him. What on earth is going on? The same Jesus who publicly declares and announces the Kingdom, the one who proclaims openly and unveils the secrets of God's reign, now strictly insists that the matter is not to be spoken of!

MESSIANIC SECRET

Jesus in Mark's gospel appears elusive, intriguing and baffling. There is a sense of obscurity. He is a paradox and an enigma. He inspires in his followers a sense of wonder and awe: "They were on the road, going up to Jerusalem, and Jesus was walking ahead of them; they were amazed" (10:32). Repeatedly, he tells his hearers *not* to speak of him. He instructs the demons who recognize him to keep silent (1:25,34; 3:11). He requires that the people he has healed do not publish his name or fame abroad (1:43ff; 5:43; 7:36; 8:26).[7]

A recurrent theme in Mark's gospel is the disciples' confusion and failure (8:17–21, 9:19). They see but do not see (8:18). The mystery of Christ is so wonderful, so potentially over-powering, so astonishing, that the disciples can only glimpse the truth little by little—like the blind man at Bethsaida who is healed by Jesus in stages: seeing first the vague shape of people, looking like walking trees, and then, later, seeing everything in clear focus (8:22–26). This becomes a symbol of the disciples' experience: they come to understand the mystery of Jesus gradually. But he has the last word: the gospel ends on a note of utter bafflement as the women flee from the disturbing empty tomb: "trembling and astonishment had come upon them" (16:8, RSV). Several times in his gospel (1:22, 6:2, 7:37, 10:26) Mark tells us that the disciples or hearers were astonished beyond measure. The Greek verb he uses, *ekpleesso*, can convey the sense that one is scared out of one's wits, frightened out of one's senses, utterly astounded or dumbfounded. Using a different, strong word the disciples are described as "being beside themselves with astonishment, stupefied" (6:51).

In Mark's gospel the themes of unveiling and concealing the mystery are interwoven and blended: Jesus is both revealer and enigma. There is so much to be revealed, so many hidden depths, that he will always remain something of a mystery even though he is partially revealed. Does this not say something powerful to us about the nature of discipleship?

Matthew's gospel gives us the parable of the hidden treasure: "The kingdom of heaven is like treasure hidden in a field, which someone found and hid; then in his joy he goes and sells all that he has and buys that field" (Matt 13:44). This saying is not found in the other gospels. It reflects the theme of searching and hiddenness that is introduced in the nativity narratives with the search of the wise men, archetypal figures representing every man and every woman in their dedicated odyssey and quest for the redeemer.

The theme of hiddenness is celebrated throughout chapter 13, where Matthew, we noted, gathers together "the secrets of the Kingdom of Heaven" (13:11). Jesus here quotes the psalmist's words: "I will open my mouth to speak in parables; I will proclaim what has been hidden from the foundation of the world" (Matt 13:35; see Ps 78:2). All vital things seem to be hidden:

- the seed, to be fruitful, must be planted deep in the earth. (Matt 13:23)

---

7. It was Wrede, of course, who first observed this in *Messianic Secret*.

- the grain of mustard seed is likewise first hidden in the soil.
- the yeast is deliberately concealed: "The kingdom of heaven is like leaven which a woman took and hid in three measures of flour." (Matt 13:33, RSV)
- "You are the salt of the earth" (Matt 5:13)—salt works invisibly.

But Jesus also says: "nothing is covered up that will not be uncovered, and nothing secret that will not become known. What I say to you in the dark, tell in the light; and what you hear whispered, proclaim from the housetops" (Matt 10:26,27). Simeon predicted: "This child is destined . . . so that the inner thoughts of many will be revealed" (Luke 2:34,35). But the paradox remains: "the kingdom of heaven is like a merchant in search of fine pearls; on finding one pearl of great value, he went and sold all that he had and bought it" (Matt 13:45,46) stands in tension with "Do not give dogs what is sacred; do not throw your pearls to pigs. If you do, they may trample them under their feet, and turn and tear you to pieces" (Matt 7:6, NIV). Yet again and again, we hear the imperative: "'Return home and tell how much God has done for you.' So the man went away and told all over town how much Jesus had done for him" (Luke 8:39).

MAKING SENSE OF THE MESSIANIC SECRET

Why the Secrecy?

Various theories have been proposed to make sense of Jesus' possible use of what we call "the messianic secret". One explanation that resonates with contemporary culture is this: Jesus did not seek to create a "celebrity cult" where people would be so-called "followers" interested only in superficial benefits like being fed freely or being relieved of Roman rule. Indeed in John 6 after the feeding of the 4000, "When Jesus realized that they were about to come and take him by force to make him king, he withdrew again to the mountain by himself" (John 6:5). Jesus comes for greater reasons and purposes, and inherited ideas about a messianic deliverer cannot contain him or force him into false categories. But in avoiding superficial popular acclaim Jesus remains an enigma and elusive.

Perhaps Paul has stumbled on the real reason Jesus might seek to escape adulation and misrepresentation. It was just not his way. He humbled himself.

> Be of the same mind, having the same love, being in full accord and of one mind. Do nothing from selfish ambition or conceit, but in humility regard others as better than yourselves. Let each of you look not to your own interests, but to the interests of others. Let the same mind be in you that was in Christ Jesus:
> though he was in the form of God,
> he did not regard equality with God as something to be exploited,
> but emptied himself taking the form of a slave,
> being born in human likeness.
> And being found in human form, he humbled himself. . .
> (Phil 2:2–8)

Pauline Writings

The writer of the letter to the Colossians weaves together the theme of treasure to be unearthed with that of the mystery of Christ. He offers this prayer: "I want their hearts to be encouraged and united in love, so that they may have all the riches of assured understanding and have the knowledge of God's mystery, that is, Christ himself, in whom are hidden all the treasures of wisdom and knowledge" (Col 2:2–3). The writer of Colossians marvels at "the mystery that has been hidden throughout the ages and generations but has now been revealed to his saints" (Col 1:26). He speaks of "the riches of the glory of this mystery, which is Christ in you, the hope of glory" (Col 1:27). He prays that his readers will gain "the riches of assured understanding and have the knowledge of God's mystery, that is, Christ himself" (Col 2:2). But while we are invited to revelation, paradoxically we are being called to hiddenness, where "your life is hidden with Christ in God" (Col 3:3).

Mystery becomes a key word in Ephesians: "God has made known to us the mystery of his will, according to his good pleasure that he set forth in Christ" (Eph 1:9); "the mystery was made known to me by revelation" (Eph 3:3); "perceive my understanding of the mystery of Christ" (Eph 3:4); "In former generations this mystery was not made known to humankind, as it has now been revealed to his holy apostles and prophets by the Spirit" (Eph 3:5).

Can the Eucharist help us to approach such mystery? As "the source and summit of the Christian life"[8] it is itself a Mount Tabor!

Eucharist—Revelation or Mystery?

> He made himself known in the breaking of bread.
> Then he vanished from their sight.

Luke 24 perfectly expresses the paradox of the Eucharist.

In the Eucharist, the veil between heaven and earth is drawn back. The *Book of Common Prayer* calls the holy communion "these holy mysteries" and reminds us that it is with angels, archangels and with the whole company of heaven that we worship the Divine: heaven and earth touch, interpenetrate and intersect at the altar. Before our very eyes physical elements become transfigured: the white host becomes filled with the Divine.[9] In the Eucharist the mystery of Christ's radiant presence astounds and astonishes the worshippers, leaving them breathless and wordless:

> Here, O my Lord, I see thee face to face;
> Here would I touch and handle things unseen . . .[10]

In the liturgies of the eastern churches the theme of revealing the holy is predominant. In the Ethiopian tradition, churches often consist of concentric circles with the holy of holies at the very center. On the altar are the *tabot*—two consecrated blocks of wood representing the tablets of the ten commandments delivered by Moses from Sinai. The Ethiopian priest will position himself on the threshold of the holy of holies and at certain points in the liturgy will push open massive double wooden doors, perhaps 20 feet tall, each bearing a colorful representation of an angel. Here the priest is literally opening the door to the sacred, and at the end of the liturgy, on certain occasions, he will joyfully bring out the *tabot*, covered in rich cloths and resting on his head: the Word of God coming once again, as it were, down the mountain and out into the center of the community. In the Syriac and Armenian traditions, the altar, which stands on a high platform or *bema*, is concealed by a richly decorated heavy curtain. This curtain is withdrawn at certain points of the liturgy, so that the worshippers can glimpse

---

8. *Catechism of the Catholic Church*, 324.

9. The platform on the altar for a monstrance for eucharistic exposition is called a Tabor.

10. Hymn by Horatius Bonar (1808–89).

heaven as represented in the altar alight with many candles. At these points when the priest pulls back the curtain, the deacons rattle their liturgical fans noisily, representing the presence of the angels. At the Great Entrance, the deacon leads a joyful procession to the altar, bearing the Eucharistic gifts of bread and wine—in a sense already holy as they have been prepared and set aside—as the sixth century Cherubic hymn is sung :

> We, who mystically represent the Cherubim,
> And chant the thrice-holy hymn to the Life-giving Trinity,
> Let us set aside the cares of life
> That we may receive the King of all,
> Who comes invisibly escorted by the Divine Hosts.[11]

The question remains, however: does the Eucharist conceal or reveal? The hymns are ambiguous, and full of paradox:

> O Jesus, by thee bidden,
> We here adore thee, hidden
> In forms of bread and wine.[12]

And yet we may proclaim of the Sweet Sacrament Divine

> in thy far depths doth shine
> thy Godhead's majesty[13]

With Thomas Aquinas himself we pray:

> O Christ, whom now beneath a veil we see,
> may what we thirst for soon our portion be:
> to gaze on thee unveiled, and see thy face,
> the vision of thy glory and thy grace.[14]

WHAT ABOUT US?

This paradox of both being known and remaining humble is a common one in Christian ministry. Clergy, for example, are encouraged to shy away from self-promotion or celebrating one's successes openly, in the name of

---

11. See also Raya, *Byzantine Liturgy*. See version "Let all mortal flesh keep silence" from Liturgy of St James in western hymnals.

12. Latin, 17th century, tr. A. Riley.

13. Stanfield (1835–1914).

14. Aquinas (1227–1274).

proper reticence or humility. But how do people discover your gifts and talent unless you in some sense "go public"? Is it possible to "go public" without emulating, in a certain way, the cult of celebrity? Is it possible to avoid self-aggrandizement or self-advertisement but at the same time allow yourself to be appreciated? And if you bury your light under a bushel you are not only creating a fire risk. You are denying glory to God. "Let your light so shine before men that they may see your good works and give glory to God in heaven" (Matt 5:16, AV). Of course we should be aware of false humility: acting humble to hide or disguise pride. This involves self-deprecation, undervaluing or belittling oneself to appear less important and make others think one is modest. What is actually happening is indirectly expressing ego, arrogance, and conceited confidence.

Since much of ministry takes place in secret, behind closed doors, the story remains untold, as confidentiality demands. There is certainly a place for reticence: it is not always appropriate to be in proclamation-mode! The writer of the first letter of Peter advises:

> All of you must clothe yourselves with humility in your dealings with one another, for "God opposes the proud, but gives grace to the humble."
> Humble yourselves therefore under the mighty hand of God, so that he may exalt you in due time. (1 Pet 5:5,6)

Theophany in Ministry?

In the practice of Christian care, we are invited to disclose the unstoppable and unconditional love of Christ. The pastoral visit becomes the locus of theophany, where God appears through the sacramentality of word or touch. In the situation being faced, we long for the disclosure of the Divine, encounter with God amidst the pain or confusion. We desire to celebrate the sacrament of divine presence in the center of everyday life, so that everything brims with God. The pastoral task becomes the privilege of stimulating and awakening our senses to the presence of Mystery; to help people become alert to the divine milieu. Thomas Merton says that the gate of heaven is everywhere: our role is to help open the door. In a sense, our task is to roll away the stone and unleash the energy and wonder of the Risen Christ.

Mystery persists

But while revelation is happening, we remain aware that we are standing only on the fringe, the brink of the Mystery: it will take a lifetime and an eternity to begin to explore. In our witness we too remain both revealer and enigma, pointing to a world, to a Divinity, as yet partially discovered.

In the Transfiguration account there is a time to speak and a time to listen. Moses and Elijah are speaking, talking with Jesus. Peter babbles forth his idea to build tents, the evangelists noting "he did not know what he was saying." But his words are heart-felt: "It is good Lord to be here." Then he must cease speaking and hear the Father's instruction: "Listen to him." As we noted, as the disciples make their way downhill, they keep silence.

The writers we have encountered in the apophatic tradition, walking the *via negativa*, caution us about being too slick when talking of God. Ultimately, we're called to nurture a sense of wonderment. We cherish the ineffability of life, content to rest in the unfathomable love of God, which is beyond comprehension; to taste the peace of God which "passes all understanding". Perhaps our greatest task is to inspire a longing and a thirst in people for something more . . . "Without any doubt, the mystery of our religion is great" (1 Tim 3:16). Recent Church of England research into the thought-world of young people puts it like this:

> At times, the mission of the Church is to make the truths of God clear, simple and accessible. At other times the mission of the Church is to spark people's curiosity . . .[15]

Jesus is both revealer and enigma. The Messianic secret persists.

FRANCISCAN HIDDENNESS AND PROCLAMATION

This tension between secrecy and openness is exemplified in the experience of the Third Order of the Society of St Francis—commonly called Tertiaries. Leading lay founder Dorothy Louise Swayne (1887—1971) was determined that members did not speak about their Franciscan life, but that it revealed itself gently through the holiness of committed lives. In her biography of Dorothy, Denise Mumford explains:

> The Third Order grew gradually, reaching 361 by 1951; numbers might have been greater had it not been for the "hiddenness,"

---

15. Savage et al, *Making Sense of Generation Y*, 117.

which was central to the ethos of the Order. Dorothy Swayne wrote in 1962: "Father Algy was insistent on the importance of hiddenness for the Third Order, and for that reason any outward badge or habit, any publicity, any talking about the Third Order to all and sundry was prohibited—hence the word 'confidential' on the outside of our Manual. We were not supposed to show this to people unless there was a very special reason for doing so." Hiddenness was an encouragement to humility, but one result was that people could not come to the Order freely, because they did not know of its existence...

A Secret Society?

This belief that the life of the spirit was extremely private originated with Dorothy's adviser Reginald Somerset Ward, arguably the most influential spiritual director of the first half of the 20th Century. She writes: "As it happens, my Director, Fr. Somerset Ward laid stress on the value of hiddenness. He himself led a totally hidden life and few people knew that such as Evelyn Underhill and William Temple were under his guidance.[16] Whenever he published a devotional book, (*The Way; Towards Jerusalem*, and so on) they were always anonymous, and he encouraged us to do the same. In this age of increasing noise and advertisement, publicity and propaganda, I do feel that this hiddenness is a very precious thing, and it will indeed be sad if the Third Order turns away from it."[17]

Dr Liz Carmichael observes: "Hiddenness was indeed a very strong theme for Somerset Ward. He saw it as essential to humility, as combatting the tendency to pride...One simply did not talk about one's inner life, it wasn't done—it would even be seen as an outright embarrassment. An obituary might just about mention that someone had a personal relationship with our Lord, but even that was a bit risqué."

In a newsletter in 1942, the issue of hiddenness had raised its head. Tertiaries were asking why they could not wear a badge, so that they could recognize each other. Dorothy wrote in response: "The mark of a Tertiary is something far more costly and far more fundamental than a metal disc—it is Humility, Love and Joy. Our Lord said much the same thing about

---

16. Michael Ramsey, Archbishop of Canterbury and Eric Abbott, Dean of Westminster were also among his directees.

17. Quotation from Swayne's letter to Father Adrian, Oct 31st, 1962 in Mumford, *Martha*, 57.

badges: 'By this you shall know that you are my disciples—if you have love for one another.'" She then wrote of humility, underlying the concept of hiddenness: "What an elusive mark this is! It is a virtue which, of its very nature, must be entirely unselfconscious. If we think we possess it, then we most certainly don't! This means that it can only begin to be achieved by the people who do not think about themselves at all, and it will certainly never be won by those who are feeling their spiritual pulse all the time. There is a self-deprecating sense of shame for personal weaknesses, and a habit of self-accusation, which we often make the mistake of regarding as humility. But this is merely inverted pride and the fruit of self-obsession. . .Humility amounts to just this: that we put no confidence in self, but unlimited confidence in God."

Make Christ Known!

Today, Franciscans take a different approach, embodied in the *Principles of the Third Order*:

> The Order is founded on the conviction that Jesus Christ is the perfect revelation of God; that true life has been made available to us through his Incarnation and Ministry, by his Cross and Resurrection, and by the sending of his Holy Spirit. The Order believes that it is the commission of the church to make the gospel known to all, and therefore accepts the duty of bringing others to know Christ, and of praying and working for the coming of the Kingdom of God.
>
> The primary aim for us as tertiaries is therefore to make Christ known.
>
> The Order sets out, in the name of Christ, to break down barriers between people and to seek equality for all.

This outward-looking approach continues to stand in some tension with a call to interiority, to nurturing the inner life:

> Our ever deepening devotion to the indwelling Christ is a source of strength and joy. It is Christ's love that inspires us to service, and strengthens us for sacrifice.
>
> We seek a deepening communion with God in personal devotion, and constantly intercede for the needs of his church and his world.

This exemplifies the tension between the mystical and the prophetic—the double call both to "guard the heart" and to engage actively with the needs of the moment. It is an expression of the call to both a contemplative and apostolic life:

> We always keep before us the example of Christ, who emptied himself, taking the form of a servant, and who, on the last night of his life, humbly washed his disciples' feet. We likewise seek to serve one another with humility.

The predominant call is to humility—but this must never become an excuse for holding back from uncomfortable duties:

> Humility confesses that we have nothing that we have not received and admits the fact of our insufficiency and our dependence upon God. . .It is the first condition of a joyful life within any community. . .We are ready to accept the lowest place when asked, and to volunteer to take it.
>
> Nevertheless, when asked to undertake work of which we feel unworthy or incapable, we do not shrink from it on the grounds of humility, but confidently attempt it through the power that is made perfect in weakness.

CHALLENGE

Ecclesiastes (3:7) reminds us: "There is time to keep silence and a time to speak." Fearlessly we must break the silence, especially if the silence becomes negative as a refusal or hesitancy to protest about a crucial issue of injustice. Are there times when we keep silent when we should speak up?

To live a transfigured life is to live within this daily paradox of involvement and detachment, availability and needful reticence. Like Jesus on Tabor, we live lives that reveal and proclaim openly the love of God, while guarding the heart, protecting inner spaces of prayer, reflection and contemplation. As Fr Silouan, an Orthodox hermit at St David's Wales, writes about the divine pattern of hide and seek:

> Transfiguration unveils the face of Christ, uncreated light and deifying glory, yet veils the revelatory Name from objectifying vanity or dualistic scrutiny. The countenance of God is unobstructed openness but remains hidden from self-interested reification. Saint Maximos the Confessor says that on Mount Tabor, the apostles

beheld Christ transfigured, who "in appearing conceals himself, in hiding manifests himself" (*Ambigua to John* 10). Revelation unveils wisdom and glory, but withholds the ineffable essence of unknowable Godhead. The Name reveals glory to wisdom but veils what the Name unveils, Godhead beyond God, whose mysteries of glory wisdom discerns. This paradox remains sheer and irreducible even when it unfolds as integral dialectic embracing veiling within unveiling. The transfigured face reflects light and glory, but conceals what it reveals to the awakened eye of the heart. It refuses itself to an objectifying stare yet gives itself to a loving gaze, a paradox which preserves the Name from the violations of vainglory. When wisdom steps back and takes in both the veiling and the unveiling as a dance of light and love, glory begins to reveal her divine play, her game of hide and seek, her playful seeking and finding. The gaze is a kiss of peace that embraces hiddenness and openness, a transfiguring gaze which embraces all in all, yet excludes all vainglorious profanations of the Holy Name. Transfiguration is wisdom's paradigm, a prism of wise discernment, well able to sort out truth from vanity.[18]

Spirituality needs to experience repeatedly a shift from the inward to the outward, and where necessary, vice versa. Jesus calls us: "whenever you pray, go into your room and shut the door and pray to your Father who is in secret" (Matt 6:6). But we also need to open the door to mission—as Paul puts it: "A wide door for effective work has opened to me, and there are many adversaries" (1 Cor 16:19); "God will open to us a door for the word, that we may declare the mystery of Christ" (Col 4:3). There is a time for closing of doors, and for flinging them wide.

QUESTIONS FOR REFLECTION

1. What does your Christian life look like when framed in terms of "revealing the holy"? What do you make of the affirmation: "Perhaps our greatest task is to inspire a longing and a thirst in people for something more..."?

2. How can we celebrate the Eucharist to emphasize the theme of "unveiling the sacred", so that the souls of participants might shimmer and quaver in awe?

---

18. Silouan, "Veiled Yet Unveiled".

3. What do you think we can learn from the Franciscans' grappling with hiddenness and proclamation?

4. How do you find yourself responding to the affirmation that Jesus is "paradox and enigma"? How do we show Jesus, messianic revelation and secret, in our lives?

5. In what particular ways do you manifest or reveal God to others?

PRAYER EXERCISE

This prayer-time is in two phases.

First, sit for a while in utter darkness. Let the darkness and silence speak to you of people's longing for God—their deep need for Christ's revelation. Also, as you quieten your heart and silence your lips, pray in the *apophaptic* mode—with wordless wonder and no attempt at describing the Divine.

Secondly, when you are ready, light a candle before you. See how the light dispels the darkness. Look at the flame and find yourself praying that you will be a radiant light in the world, revealing the wonder and mystery of Jesus to others. Pray now in the *kataphatic* mode—affirming your love for Christ, and attempting to find words to express your wonder. Pray that your light may intensify and burn ever brighter as you yourself discover more of him. Pray that epiphany may take place in your life today. End by praying Charles Wesley's great hymn:

> O Thou who camest from above, the pure celestial fire to impart
> kindle a flame of sacred love upon the mean altar of my heart.
>
> There let it for thy glory burn with inextinguishable blaze,
> and trembling to its source return, in humble prayer and fervent praise.
>
> Jesus, confirm my heart's desire to work and speak and think for thee;
> still let me guard the holy fire, and still stir up thy gift in me.
>
> Ready for all thy perfect will, my acts of faith and love repeat,
> till death thy endless mercies seal, and make my sacrifice complete.

Cloud over Tabor

5

Venturing
Between Certainty and Displacement

WE FIND OURSELVES IN a liminal space, right now. We live in an in-between time, "betwixt and between". Old paradigms are breaking down, political regimes are in revolution, banking and economic systems face unprecedented change. Technology, including the development of Artificial Intelligence, advances in leaps and bounds, leaving cherished processes obsolete. In the Church, patterns of ministry are in flux. The parish system is crumbling. Worship and liturgy are being rewritten almost daily. In post-modern society everything is questioned, and no objective truths are to be entertained.

As Hauerwas and Willimon have reminded us, we are called to live as aliens, exiles and pilgrims—that is to say, as liminal people—in this present world.[1] With the collapse of Christendom and a Constantinian model of church and state, we find ourselves in a liminal zone that is bewildering and disorientating. Old familiar landmarks are passing and we are out of our comfort zone. We can become anxious, adrift. But the liminal place is also the place of discovery, creativity, potentiality. The place of risk unleashes the power of paradox: it is discomforting but strangely renewing. In the experience of dislocation we find ourselves. Deconstruction leads to reconstruction. In the time of exile and spiritual homelessness we rediscover the heart's true home.

---

1. Hauerwas & Willimon, *Resident Aliens*.

In this chapter we reflect on how the transfigured life is lived between the poles of certainty and upheaval. We rediscover Moses and Elijah as archetypes of adventurous living. In addition, we explore how they might represent the presence of the displaced and homeless in our prayer.

MEETING REPRESENTATIVES OF THE TRADITION

"Suddenly they saw two men, Moses and Elijah, talking to him." (Luke 9:30)

Moses and Elijah enter the prayer of Jesus and he greets them and talks with them. Interpreters often say that they represent the Law and the Prophets. The phrase *the law and the prophets* refers to the entire Hebrew Scriptures: Jesus spoke of "the law and the prophets" multiple times, such as when he listed the two greatest commandments (Matt 22:40): "On these two commandments hang all the law and the prophets." In the Sermon on the Mount, Jesus says: "Do not think that I have come to abolish the Law or the Prophets; I have not come to abolish them but to fulfill them" (Matt 5:17). On the Emmaus Road, Jesus taught two disciples "everything written about himself in the Scriptures, beginning with the Law of Moses and the Books of the Prophets" (Luke 24:27, CEV).

In the context of his ministry, it seems, on initial reading, that Jesus may be consulting the sources of ancient wisdom—the Tradition. This might speak to us about the need, in times of doubt or trial, to go back to the essentials, the basics represented in the law and prophets: love for God and one another, justice, hope. The two figures can represent certainty, constancy, stability—as reliable bastions of orthodoxy, they might stand for the foundation, the touchstone, the rock—heroes and institutions of Israel's past. They are the solid, venerable guardians of historic values: John Chrysostom calls them "shining authorities."[2] Leontius in the sixth century declares "The pair Moses and Elijah are the immoveable pillars of the law."[3] They can represent the times we cling to the Tradition, our default position—something that is handed down, long-established or inherited ways of thinking or acting.

But, in fact, this phrase "the law and the prophets" is not mentioned here. Rather the focus is on the figures of Moses and Elijah themselves, and the journeys they evoke. We are told the subject of their conversation. Jesus does not talk with them about Torah. He does not discuss sacred law,

2. Daley, *Light on the Mountain*, 72.
3. Daley, *Light on the Mountain*, 126.

observances or transgressions against it. He talks about risk, danger, the laying down of his life. He will talk with them about *exodus*, as Luke 9:31 tells us:

> Their talk was about the way he must take and the end he must fulfil in Jerusalem. (Phillips)
>
> They spoke of his departure, which he was to accomplish at Jerusalem. (RSV)

The word used is not that for death (*thanatos*) but the heavily-loaded word *exodos*. It is not a death to be endured but a journey into freedom to be won. This will not just happen or occur—but will be *accomplished, fulfilled*. The word used is related to *pleroma* meaning fulness—thus we can translate: "They spoke about the journey into freedom he was to bring to completion in Jerusalem." Stevenson observes: "Transfiguration is about moving on—it is not about standing still. . .Jesus is destined to go to places no one else has been before."[4]

MEETING PILGRIMS IN TRANSIT

So, in fact, Moses and Elijah paradoxically might represent the opposite to being "establishment figures." What Moses and Elijah also have in common is that they are both displaced persons, people in transition. As John Chrysostom puts it: "God brought Moses and Elijah into glory too not that they should stay where they were but that they might even surpass their limits."

God calls us to a venturesome faith prepared to go places like Moses and Elijah. They stand before the disciples, talking about dangerous journeys, as examples of courage, as people ready to face risk and sacrifice. This is precisely what the disciples need right now, for Jesus is about to embark on his final journey and take his disciples with him, for we will soon be reading:

> They were on the road, going up to Jerusalem, and Jesus was walking ahead of them; they were amazed, and those who followed were afraid. He took the twelve aside again and began to tell them what was to happen to him, saying, "See, we are going up to Jerusalem, and the Son of Man will be handed over to the chief priests and the scribes, and they will condemn him to death; then they

---

4. Stevenson, *Detachment*, 76.

will hand him over to the Gentiles; they will mock him, and spit upon him, and flog him, and kill him; and after three days he will rise again." (Mark 10:32–34)

What the disciples—of every age—need is adventurous, daring hearts, bold, resolute spirits, readiness to follow God's leading into places or situations of risk: "God did not give us a spirit of timidity but a spirit of power and love and self-control" (2 Tim 1:7, RSV).

Moses

Moses began his life in a basket floating on the Nile—separated from his family home. He later had to quit the Pharaoh's palace and flee to Midian. Leading the exodus journey, he had to spend forty years wandering in the deserts of Sinai. He did not enter the land of promise but died on Mount Nebo, tantalizingly close but outside the boundaries of the land.

The Letter to the Hebrews celebrates Moses as a pilgrim and wayfarer:

> By faith Moses was hidden by his parents for three months after his birth, because they saw that the child was beautiful; and they were not afraid of the king's edict. By faith Moses, when he was grown up, refused to be called a son of Pharaoh's daughter, choosing rather to share ill-treatment with the people of God than to enjoy the fleeting pleasures of sin. He considered abuse suffered for the Christ to be greater wealth than the treasures of Egypt, for he was looking ahead to the reward. By faith he left Egypt, unafraid of the king's anger; for he persevered as though he saw him who is invisible. By faith he kept the Passover and the sprinkling of blood, so that the destroyer of the firstborn would not touch the firstborn of Israel. By faith the people passed through the Red Sea as if it were dry land. . . (Heb 11: 22–29)

> All of these died in faith without having received the promises, but from a distance they saw and greeted them. They confessed that they were strangers and foreigners on the earth, for people who speak in this way make it clear that they are seeking a homeland. If they had been thinking of the land that they had left behind, they would have had opportunity to return. But as it is, they desire a better country, that is, a heavenly one. Therefore God is not ashamed to be called their God; indeed, he has prepared a city for them. (Heb 11:13–16)

Gregory of Nyssa sees Moses as representing the Christian who is continually urged by God to keep moving forward. In his *Life of Moses*, as we noted, he traces a map of the Christian pilgrimage as it is suggested to him by the Exodus accounts. Ultimately this leads to the ascent of the mountain of divine knowledge, represented in Sinai.

Gregory notices that when Moses climbs a mountain he does not relax in his success but rather finds himself in a position to glimpse the further horizons and greater peaks to which God is beckoning him. From the crest, he can view the other mountains he is impelled to climb. So Gregory develops a dynamic view of spiritual development, characterized by *epekstasis*: a vision of the Christian life as continually evolving and progressing, energized by the Holy Spirit. His key text was the resolve of Paul: "Forgetting what lies behind, and straining forward (*epekteinomenos*) to what lies ahead, I press on toward the goal, for the prize of the heavenly call of God in Christ Jesus" (Phil 3:13–14). For Gregory, the disciple should never stand still, but continually stretch oneself towards the "upward call" and so reach one's full potential in Christ.[5] Each stage reached in the spiritual journey is but a beginning, not an end. Pilgrims can never say they have arrived. In Gregory's eyes, the greatest sin is that of complacency, of resting on one's laurels. From the image of Moses in transition, Gregory gains a vision of discipleship as continual adventure.

Elijah

If Moses is present as a pilgrim-figure, Elijah, too, is a displaced person, a person in transit. As the Carmelite Paul Chandler puts it: "We consider him as a man on a journey, always on the move from 'here' to 'there' in response to God's call . . . God's grace does not allow him to be still. It calls him to grow and become."[6]

Elijah's journey had taken him from the Jordan to Zarephath in the far north, from Samaria to Mount Carmel and ultimately, after a long sojourn in the desert, to Mount Horeb where he hears the still small voice of God at the mouth of the cave: God is not in the whirlwind of Elijah's life, but in quietude (1 Kgs 19:9–13). And it is precisely in the experience of stillness and solitude that Elijah receives a triple redirection of his life (19:15–17),

---

5. "On Perfection" in Musurillo, *From Glory to Glory*, 51–52. See also Louth, *Origins*.

6. Chandler, *Journey with Elijah*, 112.

and clues for the next stage of his life's journey. Mystic and activist Dorothy Soelle points out:

> [after] the experience of God in the "still, small voice" what happens now? Elijah does not withdraw into an act of worship; he does not make a pilgrimage to some shrine. Nor does he continue to divide things into the categories of sacred and profane, a division so dear to all religions. Instead, what happens is of significance for the Judeo-Christian tradition: the renewal of his political mission . . . he returns to the world.[7]

She is clear that prayer, if it involves a journey to a world within, must entail the remaking of the self—a re-energizing—so as to enable the return journey to the outer world without delay:

> The goal is to reconcile the two worlds . . . It seems almost impossible to reconcile the two: the magnitude of the inward journey which we need for experience of self, and the way back into the society of a world that can once more be lived in. Inwardness and involvement are not companion attributes in most people, for sensitive people are often not communally inclined, and people who like to be communally involved are sometimes lacking in sensitivity. Prayer and work, labor and contemplation appear to be compartmentalized into two worlds . . .
>
> The critical question with respect to expression of the deepest human experiences, those we regard as "the inward journey", is the question of connection to and with society . . . . Living as Christ lived means the inward journey to the emptying and surrendering of the ego and the return journey to the midst of this world.[8]

As we will explore in chapter 10, it is precisely in the journey within that we find an encounter not only with God but a clarification of our own identity in God, our destiny, and our vocation in the world. Thus God gives Elijah a very specific action plan, a clear set of priorities. He cannot take on everything at once; he must see what is important and what is not. The tyranny of the present moment must pass; never again must Elijah allow himself to be overwhelmed by the enormity of his task. He must be realistic, he must plan, he must pace himself. The three definite steps God requires of Elijah will in fact transform the political landscape, anointing new kings for Syria and Israel. He does not need to worry right now about precisely how Ahab

---

7. Soelle, *Inward Road*, 136.
8. Soelle, *Inward Road*, 55, 56.

and Jezebel will be removed—that is in God's hands. He must be obedient to these imperatives, and everything else can wait. In the silence of the holy mountain, Elijah regains perspective and learns to listen to God.

Called To Courage and Stamina

John Chrysostom suggests why the two great figures were invited to the theophany:

> Jesus brings Moses and Elijah on the scene, for this reason: he wanted his disciples to imitate their ability to lead, their energy, their determination...

But Jesus, looking to the future, needs his disciples to exceed and surpass their examples:

> [By the examples of Moses and Elijah] he was training the disciples in endurance by the difference in the grace that was given...For they did not go out to Egypt, but to the whole world—a far worse situation than Egypt! Nor were they simply to argue with Pharoah, but to spar with the devil, the very lord of evil! They did this not by splitting the sea in two, but by splitting the depth of wickedness, whose waves are far more terrible...Look at all the things that terrify people: death, poverty, lack of respect, countless sufferings; they trembled more at these things, than the Israelites had formerly done at the sea. Nevertheless, Jesus persuaded the disciples to take on all these dangers daringly, and to cross them, as it were, on dry land in full safety. Readying them, then, for all these challenges, he brought before them the Old Testament's shining examples.[9]

If we want to enjoy the transfiguring light of Jesus, Moses and Elijah remind us that we must also become people of courage and verve, ready for anything! We don't forget that the disciples ascending Tabor still had ringing in their ears the words of Jesus: "If any want to become my followers, let them deny themselves and take up their cross and follow me. For those who want to save their life will lose it, and those who lose their life for my sake, and for the sake of the gospel, will save it" (Mark 8:34,35).

---

9. Daley, *Light on the Mountain*, 74.

The Mountain is a Springboard for Mission

There is another feature of these two men worth noting. Moses and Elijah had both challenged tyrants and were prepared for conflict. Moses famously confronted Pharaoh, calling for the release of his people from bondage (Exod 5–12). Elijah confronts King Ahab at least twice (1 Kgs 18:17), when he predicts a drought (1 Kgs 17:1), and over King Ahab's killing of Naboth (1 Kgs 21). Their presence on the mountain heartens Jesus as he prepares for confrontation with authorities in Jerusalem, as well as reminding the disciples that conflict may be part of the journey of faith they have begun. Above all, what Moses and Elijah have in common is that Sinai/Horeb becomes a springboard for a mission dedicated to liberation from injustice. Moses' leadership of the Israelites' journey from slavery to freedom begins at the Burning Bush on Sinai; Elijah goes on to deepen and extend his struggle against idolatry and opposing forces. Through the examples of Moses and Elijah, Tabor equips us for conflict.

JESUS, ARCHETYPAL PILGRIM

Journey Between Mountains, from Tabor to Calvary

Notice how often in the Gospels Jesus is in movement, in motion. Jesus in the Gospels is radically itinerant: he doesn't settle down in his three year ministry but is always on the move. Indeed "The Son of Man has nowhere to lay his head" (Luke 9:58). Jesus is a pilgrim and wayfarer. In a sense, perhaps, he was a vagabond—which literally means a nomadic person who "wanders from place to place, without a settled home." According to Matthew's gospel, Jesus became a traveler and an exile at just a few days old, a refugee, crossing the border into Egypt.

Mark's gospel emphasizes his travels: seven times he uses the phrase "on the way"—symbol of the journey of discipleship.[10] We picture Jesus as a thirsty and dusty explorer (Luke 10:11), exhausted at times by his trek in the heat, and as a dedicated pilgrim, prepared to walk hundreds of miles to complete his journeys. Luke tells us about Jesus' pilgrimage to Jerusalem at age 12, while John gives us accounts of his pilgrim visits to the Temple for Tabernacles (Succoth) and Dedication (Hanukah) as well as the Passover celebrations in the holy city.

---

10. See Mark 8:27; 9:33–34; 10:17,32,52; 11:8.

The Jewish scholar Vermes characterizes Jesus as an itinerant Jewish charismatic[11] while Martin Hengel explores the extent to which Jesus was a wandering rabbi.[12] Scholars have noticed significances in the fact that Jesus is often on the road.[13] If Jesus had remained in Capernaum, and set up a base there for his healing ministry, establishing a center of ministry in Peter's house (Mark 1:38), this would not only limit the scope of his ministry, it would also encourage the growth of hierarchy requiring a reciprocal relationship between patrons (suppliers) and clients (those seeking healing) which was a normal feature of first century life in the Galilee. It is possible that other healers at this time set up healing sanctuaries which developed into a local personality cult. But Jesus refuses this option: by staying on the road he opens the Kingdom to a wide diversity of people throughout the region and does not put a localized limit on the range of lives he will touch and transform.

In his ministry he is peripatetic, always roving. He says: "today, tomorrow, and the next day I must be on my way" (Luke 13:33). And he is ever leading his disciples into liminal space: he leads them across borders, through boundaries, into a risky place, where they will be radically changed.

In the Gospels we see Jesus leading the disciples across the mountains of the north, to Tyre and Sidon, to the Mediterranean Sea, exposing them not only to the sea breezes but to new horizons in every sense (Mark 7). Leaving behind the comfort zone of "home", inherited prejudices, stereotypes and complacencies, the disciples discover new, unsettling and disturbing ways of seeing things, new ways of doing things, an alternative world view, represented in the Greek Syro-phoenician woman and in the woman dwelling in the no-go area of Samaria (John 4).

Later, as we noted, the disciples quit Capernaum's shoreline of safety, crossing the demon-filled sea to the Other Side, place of the Gadarene demoniacs. Jesus leads his disciples into enemy territory—into the pagan, heathen, Greek and foreign cities of the Decapolis (Matt 4:25).

We notice how Jesus takes his disciples across the desert in his final journey to Jerusalem (there is no other way between Jericho and the holy city). Here in these marginal lands of the Judean desert, the disciples discover a place of raw beauty, a wild place where the wind blasts unmercifully at times, and a place where they must be real with God.

11. Vermes, *Jesus the Jew*.
12. Hengel, *Charismatic Leader*.
13. See Crossan, *Revolutionary Biography*, 99–101.

Jesus takes his disciples across the numinous threshold of the Mount of Olives, the brink of Jerusalem, climbing up this eschatological/ "End Time" mount (Zech 14) and the threshold of the holy city. In Jerusalem Jesus will lead his disciples on journeys that culminate in the Way of the Cross, the Via Dolorosa and the pathways of resurrection.[14]

WELCOME THE DISPLACED

Unchosen Journeys

Neither Moses nor Elijah planned their journeys. They were caught up in an unfolding drama. They were responding to the demands of the moment.

On borders everywhere in the world today we find refugees: often demonized, seen as a nuisance, a threat, as invaders, as criminals fleeing justice in their homelands. Of course, in fact most are decent, honest people desperately trying to escape poverty, hunger, victimization, and violence. The scriptures strongly challenge us to welcome the stranger, immigrant and homeless. In the Hebrew scriptures we read:

> The alien who resides with you shall be to you as the citizen among you; you shall love the alien as yourself, for you were aliens in the land of Egypt: I am the Lord your God. (Lev 19:34)

> You must never do wrong things to a foreigner. Remember, you know what it is like to be a foreigner because at one time you were foreigners in the land of Egypt. (Exod 23:9 ESV)

Jesus himself begins his ministry by telling us that he has come to bring good news to the poor (Luke 4). He is emphatic, and closely identifies with the sojourner:

> When you give a feast, invite the poor, crippled, lame, blind. (Luke 13:14)

> For I was hungry and you gave me food, I was thirsty and you gave me drink, I was a stranger and you welcomed me. (Matt 25:35)

The Epistles too underline this imperative. James' words could refer, not only to the assembly, but also to the prayer space in our hearts:

---

14. I explore the other journeys in Mayes, *Beyond the Edge*, and *Roads of Hurt and Hope*.

> My brothers and sisters, do you with your acts of favoritism really believe in our glorious Lord Jesus Christ? For if a person with gold rings and in fine clothes comes into your assembly, and if a poor person in dirty clothes also comes in, and if you take notice of the one wearing the fine clothes and say, "Have a seat here, please", while to the one who is poor you say, "Stand there", or, "Sit at my feet", have you not made distinctions among yourselves, and become judges with evil thoughts? Listen, my beloved brothers and sisters. Has not God chosen the poor in the world to be rich in faith and to be heirs of the kingdom that he has promised to those who love him? (James 2:1–5)

This suggests that prayer can be for us, too, where we learn to hear the voices of the displaced, and allow them to disturb us with references to the Cross in our lives. God calls us to allow uncomfortable displaced people into our prayer space.[15] Can we welcome into our prayer the refugee, the migrant, those excluded from their homeland? This prompts us to ask these questions of our own spirituality and prayer:

- Are there danger signs that my spirituality is becoming narcissistic, self-centered, closed in on itself?
- Is my spirituality about self-fulfillment or about empowering sacrificial living?
- If the measure of spiritual maturity is increasing solidarity with the hurting, an enlarging capacity for compassion, what are the signs that I am maturing?
- Is my heart getting bigger?
- How far can I allow the pain of the world to enter my prayer? Does my prayer have room for the oppressions and injustices of the world?
- What place is there for a costly intercession which is inseparable from self-offering (and does not let me "off the hook")?
- Indeed, what is my understanding of intercession? Advising the Almighty or "coming before God with the people on your heart" (Michael Ramsey)?

---

15. I am grateful for this insight to Rowan Williams, given when I accompanied him to Tabor in 2012.

- What place is there in my prayer for the Cross—not only in terms of seeking personal forgiveness but in realizing that God suffers among us?
- What does Matthew 25 look like in my experience? What is the evidence?
- Am I drawn to the margins in any way?

Jim Wallis puts it: "Personal piety has become an end in itself instead of the energy for social justice... Prophetic spirituality will always fundamentally challenge the system at its roots and offer genuine alternatives based on values from our truest religious, cultural and political traditions."[16] A prophetic spirituality can be symbolized in hands and ears. Holy hands uplifted in prayer become hands outstretched in care, hands that may become dirty, bruised, wounded. We have, as it were, two ears: one to listen to God, one to listen to the cries of the poor, the screams of the exploited—which might turn out to be the cry of God himself.

Nomads Imprisoned

Paradoxically, today at the very foot of Mount Tabor lives a community longing for ancestral patterns of movement, but which finds its people restricted and herded. These are the Bedouin who live in the town of Shibli in Tabor's foothills. Since its inception in 1948 the State of Israel has resolved to control ancient nomadic tribes by way of "resettling" them into towns.[17] Some Bedouin have adjusted to a comfortable, risk-free, sedentary lifestyle, but many in Shibli, constituted as a town in 1992, crave their lost freedom to travel with their herds. It is foreign to their culture to live in homes of concrete rather than beneath their transitory black tents, with camels and goats nearby. Many long for the right to roam!

From Pillars to Pilgrims: Our Current Paradox

We heard Leontius declare: "The pair Moses and Elijah are the immoveable pillars of the law." But they become pilgrims, people on the road, ready for

---

16. Wallis, *Soul of Politics*, 38, 47.

17. Haaretz, "Documents Reveal Israel's Intent to Forcibly Expel the Bedouin From Their Lands."

risk, adventure and mission. What of us? Do we long with nostalgia for the "good old times" (if they ever existed!) and for the way things were, that we could depend on? Or are we ready for risk, for stepping out on unpredictable journeys, physical or metaphorical? Are we prepared to move?

The presence of Moses and Elijah on the holy mountain suggest that we need both strong foundations in our faith and a readiness to go places with God! To live a transfigured live is to remain rooted and grounded and firm in our faith while, at the same time, being ready to embrace change and challenge. The transfigured life invites us too to crave a reckless generosity of heart towards the Other.

QUESTIONS FOR REFLECTION

1. How does your prayer equip you for tough times? Have you experienced prayer as a source of courage?

2. Who have been Moses and Elijah to you in your life as people who encourage and hearten you? Are you being called to be a Moses or Elijah in the sense of being an encourager to someone facing a tough journey?

3. How have you experienced a tension between tradition and innovation/ moving forward? Is there anything that is holding you back, unnecessarily? What are the non-negotiable essentials in your faith? What are the less important things that could even be discarded, if need be? Reflect on the words:

   > May Christ dwell in your hearts through faith, as you are being rooted and grounded in love. . .To him who by the power at work within us is able to accomplish abundantly far more than all we can ask or imagine, to him be glory. . .(Eph 3:18–20)

4. In what ways do you allow the displaced of the world to enter your sacred prayer space? Do they contaminate or enrich?

5. What transitions have you experienced in society in the last 30 years? How do you find living in a world of flux?

PRAYER EXERCISE

Use the "cross-prayers" associated with Francis of Assisi. Open your arms wide—extend them as far as you can.

This is first to embody a solidarity with the Cross. Think of Jesus opening wide his arms on the Cross to embrace all who suffer, all who are in any form of distress. Think of Christ's all-encompassing love and acceptance.

Second, think of the Risen Christ and the way he longs to enfold the whole of creation, the little ones and marginalized ones of the earth.

Third, offer this prayer as an act of intercession. It is a prayer that hurts—in the sense that your arms will grow weary and ache. Moses prayed like this and needed others to hold his arms up: "Moses' hands grew weary; Aaron and Hur held up his hands, one on one side, and the other on the other side; so his hands were steady until the sun set" (Exod 17:11,12). As you feel the ache, let it connect you to those who are in pain, those who are hurting: the sick, the dispossessed, those whose human rights are trampled on.

Finally, use this prayer-action as an act of self-offering. Look at your hands that have been uplifted in prayer: who will they touch, and bless today? Offer yourself afresh to God for the part he has in store for you in his mission of reconciliation in the world.

Icon of the Transfiguration by Andrei Rublev, 1404

6

Discovering
Between Prayer and Perception

How do we actually see the world? We become conditioned to look at things in a certain way, through government information (or propaganda), through diverse media—all give us lenses through which we view things "in a certain light", as we say. The range of opinions in different newspapers, for example, tells us that there are various ways we can interpret an event. But commentators can become jaded or pessimistic, giving us a certain slant on things, a certain "take" not always helpful, and can even make us blinkered or short-sighted. We can easily get stuck in the way we make sense of certain people or events. But other perspectives are available!

Do we recognize any relationship between the way we view the world—and our own experience of prayer? Or is it "poles apart"—another dichotomy or polarization that distances one thing from another—prayer from perception? Is prayer a separate holy realm where we petition God? Or can it, in fact, be the very arena where God shapes and reshapes our thinking about the world? Have we discovered prayer as a place where we can learn to see things differently?

Before the Transfiguration Peter had become fixated on understanding Jesus as a non-suffering messiah (Mark 8:32,33)—someone in the mode of a liberating triumphant deliverer. But after the Transfiguration Peter will never again talk of Jesus in these terms—in fact, he is not recorded as calling Jesus "Messiah" after this event. Something happened on Mount Tabor that shifted his perceptions forever!

The eastern tradition of spirituality celebrates the uncreated light of Tabor—the dazzling healing light of the Transfiguration—as a key theme. But the Eastern Church considers that it is the disciples, not Christ, who are changed, in an experience akin to prayer. Here, on the mountain of prayer, their perception is enlarged, their outlook shifts, their understanding is transfigured. Lossky explains:

> The Transfiguration was not a phenomenon circumscribed in time and space; Christ underwent no change at that moment, even in his human nature, but a change occurred in the awareness of the apostles, who for a time received the power to see their Master as He was, resplendent in the eternal light of His Godhead. The apostles were taken out of history and given a glimpse of eternal realities . . . To see the divine light with bodily sight, as the disciples saw it on Mount Tabor, we must participate in and be transformed by it, according to our capacity. Mystical experience implies this change in our nature, its transformation by grace.[1]

Andreaopoulos puts it succinctly: "The real transfiguration on Tabor was not the change of Christ into something he was not before but the change of the perceptive capabilities of the apostles."[2] The change occurs in the disciples to the extent that they allow themselves to become not spectators but participants in the divinity revealed to them. Let's hear how the great eastern theologian Gregory Palamas reflects on this.

Gregory Palamas: Transformation of the Senses

> Thus, the Light of the Transfiguration of the Lord is not something that comes to be and then vanishes, nor is it subject to the sensory faculties, although it was contemplated by corporeal eyes for a short while upon a mountaintop. But the initiates of the Mystery, the disciples of the Lord at this time passed beyond mere flesh into spirit through a transformation of their senses, effected within them by the Spirit, and in such a way that they beheld what, and to what extent, the divine Spirit had wrought blessedness in them to behold the Ineffable Light. . .
>
> That same inscrutable Light shone and was mysteriously manifest to the Apostles and the foremost of the Prophets at that moment, when the Lord was praying. This shows that what

---

1. Lossky, *Mystical Theology*, 22.
2. Andreopoulos, *Metamorphosis*, 71.

brought forth this blessed sight was prayer, and that the radiance occurred and was manifest by uniting the mind with God, and that it is granted to all who, with constant exercise in efforts of virtue and prayer, strive with their mind towards God. True beauty, essentially, can be contemplated only with a purified mind. To gaze upon its luminance assumes a sort of participation in it, as though some bright ray etches itself upon the face. . .

In the teachings of the Fathers, Jesus Christ was transfigured on the Mount, not taking upon Himself something new nor being changed into something new, nor something which formerly He did not possess. Rather, it was to show His disciples that which He already was, opening their eyes and bringing them from blindness to sight. For do you not see that eyes that can perceive natural things would be blind to this Light?

Thus, this Light is not a light of the senses, and those contemplating it do not simply see with sensual eyes, but rather they are changed by the power of the divine Spirit. They were transformed, and only in this way did they see the transformation taking place amidst the very assumption of our perishability, with the deification through union with the Word of God in place of this. . .

How otherwise could the Apostles recognize those whom they had never seen before [Moses and Elijah], unless through the mysterious power of the divine Light, opening their mental eyes?[3]

Unfettering Spiritual Eyes

Gregory delights in the theme of discovery of the Divine on Tabor: it is not so much that Jesus was changed in the event of the Transfiguration, but that the perception of the disciples was enlarged—they learned to see things differently. This echoes Luke's account: "Now Peter and his companions were weighed down with sleep; *but when they were fully awake* they saw his glory (9:32). This is not only a physical stirring but an awakening of their spiritual senses and an expansion of their capacity to sense the Divine, the gift of a new perception, new alertness, a transformation of their senses, effected within them by the Spirit. Now they can see the unseen, and comprehend the incomprehensible. Gregory can hardly contain his excitement when he says that we all have the potential for such a sensing of the Divine: "This

---

3. "St. Gregory Palamas: Homily on the Transfiguration" in Daley, *Light on the Mountain*.

shows that what brought forth this blessed sight was prayer, and that the radiance occurred and was manifest by uniting the mind with God, and that it is granted to all who, with constant exercise in efforts of virtue and prayer, strive with their mind towards God."

In his work *The Triads* Gregory quotes John Damascene: "Christ is transfigured, not by putting on some quality He did not possess previously, nor by changing into something He never was before, but by revealing to His disciples what He truly was, in opening their eyes and in giving sight to those who were blind. For while remaining identical to what He had been before, He appeared to the disciples in His splendor; He is indeed the true light, the radiance of glory."[4] This mysterious light, inaccessible, immaterial, uncreated, deifying, eternal, this radiance of the divine nature, this glory of the divinity, this beauty of the heavenly kingdom, is at once accessible to sense perception and yet transcends it.[5]

The mystery of Mount Tabor tells us then that there are different ways of seeing. There is natural sensing and also spiritual perception, seeing as it were another dimension that can be easily missed. The event of Mount Tabor is at once an unveiling and divine disclosure and an unleashing and unfettering of human faculties, an unlocking of shuttered inner eyes. Christ permanently reveals his glory; he does not hide it. It is our disbelief and spiritual blindness that limit us and hold us back from perceiving the divine shining of Christ's glory. We are challenged to live with a heightened sense of awareness and alertness to the Divine, which is enabled by a synergy of our longing and commitment and the working in us of the Holy Spirit.

Such illumination and enlightenment, bringing the deepest kind of spiritual knowledge comes, teaches Gregory, through *theoria*. Andrew Louth explains:

> The word *theoria* is derived from a verb meaning to look, or to see: for the Greeks, knowing was a kind of seeing, a sort of intellectual seeing. Contemplation is, then, knowledge, knowledge of reality itself, as opposed to knowing how: the kind of know-how involved in getting things done. To this contrast between the active life and contemplation, there corresponds a distinction in our understanding of what it is to be human, between . . . puzzling things out, solving problems, calculating and making decisions. . . and being receptive of truth, beholding, looking—referred to by the Greek words *theoria* or *sophia* (wisdom) or *nous* (intellect). . . Human

4. Palamas, *Triads*, 76.
5. Palamas, *Triads*, 81.

intelligence operates at two levels: a basic level concerned with doing things, and another level concerned with simply beholding, contemplating, knowing reality.[6]

Palamas teaches that today we can experience for ourselves a vision of divine radiance that is the same light that was manifested to Jesus' disciples on Mount Tabor at the Transfiguration. Such *theoria* is enabled by the Holy Spirit, first given in baptism and fostered by participation in the sacraments of the Church, the performance of works of faith and above all by prayer.

PRAYER AND PERCEPTION

Reflecting on the meaning of Mount Tabor, Gregory raises for us questions about perception: how we look at things, what we actually see. Gregory prompts us to ask: is the glory of God actually in front of our eyes but we just don't see? He is emphatic that the transformation on Tabor was the change in the disciples' eyes and their heightened capacity to see. The key for Gregory in regaining this lost capacity to sense the Divine is the prayer of stillness and silence—this makes possible a state of receptivity enabling a contemplative way of looking at the world. He says in his sermon, as we noted: "what brought forth this blessed sight was prayer."

A number of recent writers talk of prayer as means of perception and as a way of knowing. Moltmann contrasts two approaches in epistemology. In modern scientific methods, he maintains, we know in order to achieve mastery, to gain possession of our subject. But there is a second way:

> Meditation is in fact an ancient method of arriving at knowledge which has not been pushed aside by our modern activism. . .meditation is pre-eminently a way of sensory perception, of receiving, of absorbing and participating. . .The act of perception transforms the perceiver . . . Perception confers communion. We know in order to participate, not in order to dominate.[7]

For John Macquarrie, prayer helps to heal the human experience of fragmentedness and individualistic isolation, enabling the pray-er to see the world as a whole: "prayer enables us to see things in perspective. . .Prayer changes our vision of the world. . .Prayer interprets the world."[8] Rowan

---

6. Louth, "Theology, Contemplation and the University".
7. Moltmann, *Spirit of Life*.
8. Macquarrie, *Paths in Spirituality*, 34.

Williams describes contemplative prayer as involving "the project of reconditioning perception."[9]

Watts and Williams in their study *The Psychology of Religious Knowing* are cautious about assigning a directly cognitive role to prayer, but they recognize significant shifts in perception taking place in the practice of prayer: "Indeed it is doubtful whether the 'acquisition of knowledge' is at all an appropriate way to describe the cognitive changes that take place in prayer. Prayer is probably better described as the *reinterpretation* of what is in some sense already known than as an exercise in the acquisition of knowledge."[10] For Williams and Watts, prayer is "an exercise in the interpretation of experience."[11]

Prayer, especially the quiet, reflective type, becomes the place where perspicacity and real discernment is possible, where we see things with fresh eyes. A. and B. Ulanov in *Primary Speech: A Psychology of Prayer* write of the transformations in perception that can take place in the course of prayer:

> This means we are living now in rearranged form. We are the same persons and yet radically different. . .The theme that dominates our lives now is the effort to correspond with grace. We want to go with the little signs and fragments of new being given us in prayer.[12]

Thus prayer entails the risk of change, in which, little by little, perceptions are revised, self-acceptance grows, and contradictions, if not resolved, become better understood. Effective prayer is, then, not about seeking to influence God, but about allowing God to do extraordinary things in us. This questions our contemporary practice of prayer. It requires of us the ability to silence our own admonitions and advice-giving to God, which can be a feature of intercessory prayer (as if we were advising the Almighty what he should do next). It requires us to come to a place of vulnerability and receptivity before God—a wakefulness that the disciples discovered on Tabor.

---

9. Williams, *Teresa of Avila*, 156.

10. Watts & Williams, *Religious Knowing*, 115.

11. Watts & Williams, *Religious Knowing*, 113. Attribution theory, religious people attributing events to God, helps to understand this process.

12. Ulanov, *Primary Speech*, 122. Experiences of God as perception in Alson, *Perceiving God*.

Seeing Sacramentally

The Fourth Gospel does not include an account of the Transfiguration, unlike the other three—perhaps because the themes of perception and transfiguration are on every page. Throughout the fourth gospel, Jesus is seeking eyes wide open. He begins his ministry with the summons, the invitation: "Come and see" (1:39). Jesus wants to open the disciples to a new vision and a fresh way of seeing reality. He calls them to become wide awake to the possibilities God is opening up. He challenges their perception of things. "Do you not say, 'There are yet four months, then comes the harvest'? I tell you, lift up your eyes, and see how the fields are already white for harvest" (John 4:35, RSV). But he is not talking about Samaritan agriculture. The fields around them speak to Jesus of the growth of the Kingdom and the spiritual harvest which has become imminent. In chapter 9 John teaches us about true sight, far deeper than natural eyesight—it is about discerning and recognizing the Divine.

A sacramental way of viewing reality is a dominant theme in the fourth gospel. Jesus sees wine, vines, water, bread, sunlight and candlelight, even shepherding as speaking of himself. Jesus looks at a seed and sees its potential if it perishes: "unless a grain of wheat falls into the earth and dies, it remains just a single grain; but if it dies, it bears much fruit" (12:24). He glimpses his very destiny in a kernel of wheat.

The other gospels combine to give us the clear impression that this was an outlook on the world that was truly characteristic of Jesus himself. The secrets of the Kingdom reveal themselves through parables of seed, mountain, field and sea (Matt 13, Mark 11:23). Jesus says: "Consider the lilies, how they grow . . ." (Luke 12: 27). "Consider": the Greek word means "turn your attention to this, notice what is happening, take note." It is a summons to a contemplative way of life, a deeply reflective way of seeing the world.

To live a transfigured life requires that we give up on narrow, prescriptive, hectoring types of prayer. It invites us to be poised and ready in times of prayer to be changed, to be aware that we might be standing on the brink of new discoveries of the Gospel. It invites us to be set to shift perceptions of the Divine.

QUESTIONS FOR REFLECTION

1. What is your experience of perceptions shifting during the course of prayer? How do you find yourself responding to Gregory's take on the Transfiguration—the change in the disciples' ability to see?

2. What do you make of the observations from Macquarrie, Moltmann and Rowan Williams? Do you agree with them?

3. The glory is always there, seemingly veiled. How can we train ourselves to hone our ability to see deeply, beneath the surface, to recognize the Divine in our very midst, to live in such a way that we might glimpse more of Divinity in the world? God's presence is here before us now—are we seeing it or missing it? How would you assess your own awareness of the Divine?

4. Consider a situation you face right now. See if you can look at it differently. Dare you pray: "Lord, show me your glory"? As you prayerfully reflect, revisit your assumptions and interpretations of people and events.

5. Look up Psalms 22 and 42. Notice how the psalmist's perceptions shift during the course of his prayer, and how he ends up in a different place, as it were, at the end compared with how he was at the beginning. What other examples in the psalms can you find? Which resonate most with your own experience?

PRAYER EXERCISE

Anglican poet-priest George Herbert (1593–1633) shows us how perceptions can alter during the experience of praying, his poems conveying "a picture of the many spiritual conflicts that have passed betwixt God and my soul." They testify to an on-going struggle to accept personally within himself God's unconditional love. He wrestled with a sense of spiritual confusion, the dilemma of unanswered prayer. He discovered prayer to be a place of utter transparency before God: as we come before God just as we are, we lower our self-protective barriers, those shields we put up to sheathe ourselves from others. Herbert comes before God with all his woundedness and fragility, prepared to speak out his questions and give voice to his vulnerability. The prayer-time becomes a liminal place of transformation.

He is undone and remade. In *Longing* he lays bare his soul's paradoxes, and confesses that to him God seems absent, aloof, faraway, and unresponsive, but his prayer becomes a pilgrimage in paradox towards a new sense that all is well. Herbert sees that his questions and the experience of being pulled in different directions all meet in the Cross. Indeed, on the Cross God has already enfolded and experienced them; he has *felt* them:

> Ah, my dear Father, ease my smart!
> These contrarieties crush me: these Cross actions
> Do wear a rope about, and cut my heart:
> And yet since these thy contradictions
> Are properly a Cross felt by thy Son,
> With but four words, my words, *Thy will be done*.[13]

Herbert teaches us about movement in prayer: a movement from questions, burdens, struggles to a place of surrender, an end to resisting.[14] Famously, in *Love III* he leaves behind a sense of unworthiness and arrives at a place where he experiences acceptance, giving in to God. Repeatedly he discovers that it is at the point of submission, paradoxically, that we discover God's empowerment.[15]

Reflect on how your moods and perceptions sometimes shift during times of prayer. Conclude with Herbert's poem:

> Love bade me welcome. Yet my soul drew back
>   Guilty of dust and sin.
> But quick-eyed Love, observing me grow slack
>   From my first entrance in,
> Drew nearer to me, sweetly questioning,
>   If I lacked any thing.
>
> A guest, I answered, worthy to be here:
>   Love said, You shall be he.
> I the unkind, ungrateful? Ah my dear,
>   I cannot look on thee.
> Love took my hand, and smiling did reply,
>   Who made the eyes but I?

---

13. Herbert, *Works*. See also, Mayes, *Spirituality of Struggle*; Sheldrake, *Love Took My Hand*.

14. *The Collar* transits from desperation to affirmation; *Evensong* moves from failure to a fresh perspective.

15. Poems available on www.ccel.org

>   Truth Lord, but I have marred them: let my shame
>   Go where it doth deserve.
>   And know you not, says Love, who bore the blame?
>   My dear, then I will serve.
>   You must sit down, says Love, and taste my meat:
>   So I did sit and eat.

Pray—or sing!—Herbert's prayer *The Elixir* to recognize the Divine everywhere:

> Teach me, my God and King, / In all things Thee to see,
> And what I do in anything / To do it as for Thee.
>
>   A man that looks on glass, / On it may stay his eye;
> Or if he pleaseth, through it pass, / And then the heav'n espy.
>
>   All may of Thee partake: / Nothing can be so mean,
> Which with his tincture—"for Thy sake"—/Will not grow bright and clean.
>
>   A servant with this clause / Makes drudgery divine:
> Who sweeps a room as for Thy laws, /Makes that and th' action fine.
>
>   This is the famous stone / That turneth all to gold;
> For that which God doth touch and own / Cannot for less be told.

Light above Tabor Basilica

7

Journeying
Between Local and Cosmic

THE TRANSFIGURATION EVENT STRETCHES us between a local mountain in the Galilee region and the entire cosmos! We are invited to climb the steep wooded slopes of the Galilean mountain of Tabor with Jesus and the disciples—and contemplate the entire universe as it is revealed in the Transfiguration. We reflect here on the tension between being committed to the local, and openness to the immensity of space, the infinity of creation. How can we be committed to the needs and joys of our own community without becoming parochial or confined in our outlook? How can we somehow carry within us the widest perspectives, cosmic vision, as we go about our daily lives? How can we be attentive to the wondrous details of creation without being absorbed by minutiae in a restricting or inward-looking sense? How can our world view encompass the micro and the macro? How do we hold our competing concerns—local and global—within a life-giving tension, and without being torn apart?

Sometimes the Christian vision can become narrowed. Some focus on understanding first century Palestine in order to set Jesus of Nazareth in context, but he gets, as it were, imprisoned there. Others might focus on Jesus devotionally in such a way that an individualistic "Jesus and me" mentality takes hold. Someone[1] once wrote a book called "Your God Is

---

1. J.B. Phillips

Too Small." How does the Transfiguration draw us between the historical figure of Jesus and the Christ filling the universe?

In this chapter we shift from Jesus of Nazareth to the Cosmic Christ, as we retrieve and reconnect to the staggering tradition of the Christ that transcends heaven and earth. We will find this opens before us a breadth of vision that is breathtaking, mind-boggling, stupendous.

Icons—Compass to Wider Vision

In iconography of the Transfiguration a distinctive feature is the circle in which the radiant figure of Christ stands: akin to the mandala found in many religious traditions, this is often called the mandorla. The mandorla (Italian: "almond") is an almond-shaped aureole of light; as a circle, iconographically the most perfect shape, it symbolizes the fountainhead of the Divine. Andreopoulos explains:

> The round mandorla suggests that the Transfiguration was a metaphysical event in which heaven revealed itself through Christ. Moreover, Christ, as the center of the circle, revealed his position as the center of all the oppositions and balances that this circular mandorla may signify. . .the image of Christ as a mandorla has a strong cosmic dimension. The incarnate God, who reveals no less than heaven in his Transfiguration, is not very different from the image of Christ *Pantokrator*.[2]

In addition, as in the icon of Theophanes the Greek's icon, six triangles radiate out from the circle: they represent the explosion and effulgence of divine uncreated light emanating from Christ to all points of the universe: the rays of light issuing forth from their points penetrate the whole cosmos. The Transfiguration, the icons declare, is a cosmic event touching and renewing the furthest bounds of creation. The mandorla and the broad "light rays" emanating from Jesus in such icons are details that go back to the earliest known Transfiguration image in St. Catherine's monastery on Mount Sinai (6th century). The rays escaping from Christ's radiant body indicate the sun, their golden lines touching heaven and earth expressing the transmission of the divine energy to the ends of the earth—and beyond!

---

2. Christ, the Ruler of All, as depicted in domes of Orthodox churches. Andreopoulos, *Metamorphosis*, 146.

The white as a symbol of light has the attribute of spreading as it drives through space. As such it represents what is timeless.[3]

Christ is more than just an historical person who walked this earth for 33 years, a great teacher and miracle-worker. A wider vision enables us to glimpse Jesus the Christ as the Alpha and the Omega, filling all things. The Christology or image of Christ that predominates in our thinking and devotion will have a great impact on our view of mission. Is mission a question of seeking more disciples and followers for Jesus of Nazareth? Or might it involve a commitment to the very cosmos we inhabit?

In this chapter, first we look at biblical material, as we ponder the meaning "the Word made flesh." We engage with the cosmic Christ celebrated in early Christian hymns preserved in the New Testament. Second, we will hear voices from the history of Christian spirituality. Thirdly, we attend to contemporary or recent writers.

1 DISCOVERING THE COSMIC CHRIST IN THE NEW TESTAMENT

Awesome passages in the New Testament expand our consciousness and point us to a more expansive view of Jesus of Nazareth. Significantly, this cosmic understanding of Christ is found in different authors and across different communities.

John's Gospel: The Word Was Made Flesh

> In the beginning was the Word, and the Word was with God, and the Word was God. He was in the beginning with God. All things came into being through him, and without him not one thing came into being. What has come into being in him was life, and the life was the light of all people. . .And the Word became flesh and lived among us, and we have seen his glory (John 1:1–3,14).

Scholars have long debated the background to John's use of *Logos*, the Word. What does John wish us to keep in mind as he writes of the role of the Word in the creation of the world, the Word that in the fullness of time will be enfleshed and embodied in the person of Jesus? Some point to the Greek background—this emphasizes the solemn and serious import of

---

3. See Tippett, "The Transfiguration by Theophanes the Greek".

the word *Logos*—it represents the rational principle, ensuring order and stability in creation. In Stoic philosophy *Logos* connotes the structuring principle of the universe, a formal abstraction behind created reality. Greek philosophers like Philo thought of the *Logos* as representing divine reason and logic, bringing order into the midst of chaos. It is a staid and stolid approach.

But the Hebrew background to the *Logos* points us to the mysterious, creative and playful Wisdom of God. Ecclesiasticus celebrates God's *Sophia*:

> I came forth from the mouth of the Most High, and covered the earth like a mist.
> I dwelt in the highest heavens, and my throne was in a pillar of cloud.
> Alone I compassed the vault of heaven and traversed the depths of the abyss.
> Over waves of the sea, over all the earth, over every people and nation
> I have held sway. (Sirach 24: 3–6)

The *Logos* in the Hebrew Scriptures represents God's playmate in the act of creation, God's Wisdom, evoking a joyful, frisky, gamboling, dancing playfulness in the heart of God. Proverbs 8 puts it:

> The LORD created me at the beginning of his work,
>   the first of his acts of long ago.
> Ages ago I was set up,
>   at the first, before the beginning of the earth.
> When there were no depths I was brought forth,
>   when there were no springs abounding with water.
> Before the mountains had been shaped,
>   before the hills, I was brought forth—
> when he had not yet made earth and fields,
>   or the world's first bits of soil.
> When he established the heavens, I was there,
>   when he drew a circle on the face of the deep,
> when he made firm the skies above,
>   when he established the fountains of the deep,
> when he assigned to the sea its limit,
>   so that the waters might not transgress his command,
> when he marked out the foundations of the earth,
>   then I was beside him, like a little child
> and I was daily his delight,
>   playing before him always,
> rejoicing in his inhabited world
>   and delighting in the human race.

Here's a dynamic and vibrant view of the *Logos*: the one who is rejoicing in the playfulness of creation, as a little child delights in making new things, crafting and shaping materials. Such an energy, a verve, a daring, a passionate life-force shimmering throughout creation, a sparkling vitality—this is now to be embodied in the person of Jesus. But the "scandal of particularity"—God incarnate in Jesus of Nazareth—requires a geography...

The Local and the Universal

We turn from the Synoptics for a moment to John's gospel because it powerfully reveals the paradox we face as we seek to balance in our spiritual practice the local and the universal, the particular and the cosmic. From the outset, it reveals an acute sense of place. "Come and see"—this summons resounds across the gospel. We are invited in the fourth gospel to accompany Jesus as he traverses the land as a pilgrim and traveler. We get a sense that the author of the fourth gospel has a first-hand knowledge of the land, its valleys and plains. Bruce Schein observes: "John has probably been the most neglected Gospel in terms of the touchable and seeable background of the first century... John constantly keeps the reader informed with precise geographical data... To enter into this 'feeling' with and for the land with eyes, ears, hands, and hearts is important for a complete understanding of the Johannine setting."[4]

John has a sharp eye, a fascination, for the details, keen attentiveness to physicality and environment. He tells us the well is deep, and it is in a field (4:5,11). There is a lot of water at Aenon near Salim (3:23). Grass covers hills above Sea of Galilee (6:10). Lazarus tomb is a cave (11:38). The tomb of Jesus has a low entrance (they stooped to look in, 20:5). We learn details about the Jerusalem temple: forecourts accommodate a range of animals (2:13–16); the porticoes of Solomon offer shelter in winter (10: 22,23); the treasury is a suitable place for teaching (8:20). John takes us to visit the Bethesda, describing a pool near the Sheep Gate with five colonnades or porticos (a line of columns supporting a roof-like structure, 5:2). He gives special significance to the Pool of Siloam (9:1–9). The first is north of the temple, the other south, and both function in relation to the temple. He tells us that the house of the High Priest has a courtyard, with a fire in it (18:5,18). John records that Jesus was crucified at Golgotha, the place of the skull, which was located "near the city", meaning just outside the city

---

4. Schein, *Following the Way*, 7, 8.

walls (19:13). Uniquely, he tells us that there is a garden close by, in which an unused tomb had been carved into the rock (19:41–42). We even learn that there is an inviting beach on the shore of Lake Galilee (21)!

While celebrating this alertness to the local and the particular, it is important to recall that all is set within a cosmic perspective: literally so, for when John speaks of the world he uses the word *cosmos*. For John, there is a paradox in this widest of settings. The world is the object of God's love: "For God so loved the world that he gave his only Son" (3:16). He goes on: "In the world you face persecution. But take courage; I have conquered the world!" (16:33). John's prologue alerts us to this: "The true light, which enlightens everyone, was coming into the world. He was in the world, and the world came into being through him; yet the world did not know him" (1:9,10). Moving between intimacy and ultimacy, John invites us to appreciate the smallest details of place without losing a sense of the bigger picture—of cosmic dimensions! In the fourth gospel, Jesus is at once the dusty pilgrim and traveler traversing the land, and the very creator Word made flesh!

In today's frantic world we lose a sense of time and place, of sacred space. Globalization and standardization mean we may become less attentive to the small picture, the local, the particular and peculiar.

New Testament Hymns Celebrate the Cosmic Christ

Paul's vision is that God will be "all in all" (1 Cor 15:28).

The Letter to the Philippians preserves an early hymn that gives us a glimpse into the increasing expansiveness of vision and understanding experienced by the first Christians:

> He humbled himself
>   and became obedient to the point of death—even death on a Cross.
> Therefore God also highly exalted him
>   and gave him the name that is above every name,
> so that at the name of Jesus every knee should bend,
>   in heaven and on earth and under the earth,
> and every tongue should confess that Jesus Christ is Lord,
>   to the glory of God the Father. (Phil 2: 5–11)

In this great poem the first Christians hold together in a taut tension the historical reality of Jesus of Nazareth and a cosmic view of his divinity. Within a few lines the brutality of the crucifixion is recalled as the centerpoint of history moving to a cosmic worshipping of Christ. The hymn challenges us to hold together the historical and the cosmic in the same breath, and never to see the Cross in terms of a local crucifixion without the wider, mind-boggling perspective and expansiveness of vision.

"Every knee should bend, in heaven and on earth and under the earth": Paul's hymns evoke the Hebrew Bible's three-part world, with the heavens (*shamayim*) above, earth (*eres*) in the middle, and the underworld (*sheol*) below. In the Old Testament the word *shamayim* represented both the sky/atmosphere, and the dwelling place of God. The *raqia* or firmament—the visible sky—was a solid inverted bowl over the earth, colored blue from the heavenly ocean above it.

Other strands in the New Testament push out the boundaries of our thinking about the person of Christ. Some envisage multiple heavens.

The Letter to the Hebrews celebrates:

> We have a great high priest who has passed through the heavens, Jesus, the Son of God. (Heb 4:14)

> It was fitting that we should have such a high priest, holy, blameless, undefiled, separated from sinners, and exalted above the heavens. (Heb 7:26)

It sets before us a colossal image in its opening words:

> Long ago God spoke to our ancestors in many and various ways by the prophets, but in these last days he has spoken to us by a Son, whom he appointed heir of all things, through whom he also created the worlds. He is the reflection of God's glory and the exact imprint of God's very being, and he sustains all things by his powerful word.

The Letter to the Ephesians speaks of Christ filling multiple heavens in its hymn:

> He has let us know the mystery of his purpose,
> the hidden plan he so kindly made in Christ from the beginning
> to act upon when the times had run their course to the end:
> that he would bring everything together under Christ, as head,
> everything in the heavens and everything upon earth
> (Eph 1:9–10, JB)

The letter offers the grounds and basis for hope:

> This you can tell from the strength of his power at work in Christ, when he used it to raise him from the dead and made him sit at

his right hand, in heaven, far above every Sovereignty, Authority, Power, or Domination, or any other name that can be named, not only in this age but also in the age to come. He has put all things under his feet, and made him, as the ruler of everything, the head of the Church; which is his Body, the fullness of him who fills the whole creation. (Eph 1:17–23)

In cosmic language, the Letter to the Ephesians celebrates Christ filling all things: "He who descended is the same one who ascended far above all the heavens, so that he might fill all things" (Eph 4:10).

Colossians in its poem opens before our imagination the widest horizons:

> He is the image of the unseen God
> and the first-born of all creation,
> for in him were created
> all things in heaven and on earth:
> everything visible and everything invisible,
> Thrones, Dominations, Sovereignties, Powers –
> all things were created through him and for him.
> Before anything was created, he existed,
> and he holds all things in unity . . .
> God wanted all perfection to be found in him
> and all things to be reconciled through him and for him,
> everything in heaven and everything on earth . . .
> (Col 1:15–17,19–20, JB)

Compare translations of the key text Colossians 1:17

> He is before all, and all things subsist together by him. (Darby)

> He Himself existed and is before all things, and in Him all things hold together. His is the controlling, cohesive force of the universe. (AMP)

2 CHRISTIAN THEOLOGIANS AND MYSTICS DISCOVER A COSMIC CHRIST

Throughout the history of Christian spirituality mystics and teachers have expanded our consciousness of the person of Christ.

Theologians of the Fourth and Fifth Centuries

Seeking to counter a watered-down understanding of Christ as espoused by Arius, outstanding defenders of the faith affirm that Christ is the eternally pre-existent Word of God. They embody their convictions in the Nicene Creed of 325:

> We believe in one Lord, Jesus Christ, the only Son of God,
> eternally begotten of the Father,
> God from God, Light from Light, true God from true God,
> begotten, not made, of one Being with the Father.
> Through him all things were made.
> For us and for our salvation he came down from heaven:
> by the power of the Holy Spirit he became incarnate from the Virgin Mary,
> and was made man...

The cosmic Christ reveals the meaning of the universe. **Basil of Caesarea** (329–378) declares: "The Word of God pervades the creation." **Gregory of Nazianzus** (329–390) says: "This name *Logos* was given to him because he exists in all things that are." **Athanasius of Alexandria** (296–373) speaks of "The Logos of God who is over all and who governs all."[5] In his great book *Christus Victor* Gustaf Aulen celebrates the classic approach to the Cross which is seen as a battlefield where Christ takes on and defeats humanity's greatest foes and negative, destructive forces: the forces of sin and death, indeed everything that threatens, erodes and undermines the integrity of the cosmos and contributes to its degradation.

Mystics of the Medieval Period

Hildegard of Bingen (1098–1179), poet, mystic and musician leads us into the medieval period. Today we talk about the "greening of the planet" but nine hundred years ago Hildegard celebrated the presence of the Holy Spirit in the created order through the idea of greening or *viriditas*: "the earthly expression of the celestial sunlight; greenness is the condition in which earthly beings experience a fulfillment which is both physical and divine; greenness is the blithe overcoming of the dualism between earthly and heavenly."[6] For Hildegard, the wetness or moisture of the planet, revealed in verdant growth, bespeaks the Holy Spirit who "poured out this

---

5. Quotes drawn from Pelikan, *Jesus Through the Centuries*, ch. 5.
6. Peter Dronke, quoted in Bowie & Davies, *Hildegard of Bingen*, 32.

green freshness of life into the hearts of men and women so that they may bear good fruit".[7] She invites us to see the world differently, overcoming the dichotomy of heaven and earth by glimpsing the heavenly action in the freshness of the planet, which mirrors the human soul. We are being summoned away from a pragmatic and self-centered consumer mentality, so deeply entrenched in our culture and mind-set, towards seeing creation as not an entity to be manipulated or exploited but a divine presence to be honored. Hildegard hears Christ say to her:

> I, the fiery life of divine wisdom,
> I ignite the beauty of the plains,
> I sparkle the waters,
> I burn in the sun, and the moon, and the stars,
> With wisdom I order all rightly...
> I adorn all the earth.
> I am the breeze that nurtures all things green...
> I am the rain coming from the dew
> That causes the grasses to laugh with the joy of life.[8]

Mechtild of Magdeburg (1210–1280) in her mystical Beguine book *The Flowing Light of the Godhead* combines intense personal love for Christ with a cosmic view. He is both bridegroom and lover of the soul and also cosmic Lord: here again, intimacy meets ultimacy. Mechtild expresses the paradoxes in Christology: Jesus among us is a pilgrim trudging across the world, a poor worker, but also omnipresent Lord.[9] In prayer she addresses Christ in tender terms:

> You are the feelings of love in my desire.
> You are a sweet cooling for my breast.
> You are a passionate kiss for my mouth.
> You are a blissful joy of my discovery.

She also shares with us her awesome, expansive vision:

> One day I saw with the eyes of my eternity
> In bliss and without effort, a stone.
> This stone was like a great mountain
> And was of assorted colors.
> It tasted sweet, like heavenly herbs.

7. Bowie & Davies, *Hildegard of Bingen*, 32. See Craine, *Hildegard*, 26–27.
8. Uhlein, *Meditations*, 31. Another translation in Fox, *Book of Divine Works*, 8. See also Fox, *Cosmic Christ*, 110.
9. Tobin, *Mechtild of Magdeburg*, 286, 284.

> I asked the sweet stone: who are you?
> It replied: "I am Jesus."[10]

She delights in the imagery of the Sun:

> The sparkling sun of the living Godhead
> Shines through the bright water of cheerful humanity...
> You shine into my soul
> Like the sun against gold.

And she hears God responding:

> When I shine, you shall glow.
> When I flow, you shall become wet.[11]

Franciscan Tradition

This opens us to a dual perspective of the micro and macro.

Francis of Assisi (1181–1226) can attend to the tiniest details around him—famously, he picked up worms to move them out of harm's way—while having his sights on the heavens:

> Praise God, Brother Sun!
> Beautiful and radiant with great splendor,
> you bear a likeness of the Most High!
> Praise God, Sister Moon and stars,
> God formed you in heaven clear and precious and beautiful!
> Praise God, Sister Water!
> God made you useful, humble, precious and chaste.
> Praise God, our Sister Mother Earth!
> you govern and sustain us,
> with fruit and colors, flowers and herbs.
> Let the universe praise and bless my God and give God thanks
> and serve with great humility!

Moreover, Francis glimpsed the inter-connectedness of all things—that all things belong together. He rejected the narrow materialist capitalist view of his merchant-father, who personified a grasping exploitative approach to "things." Rather he came to appreciate that all elements in creation, animate and inanimate, can be greeted as brother or sister.

10. Woodruff, *Meditations*, 108.
11. Tobin, *Mechthild*, 152, 76.

Bonaventure (1221–1274) observes: "When Francis considered the primordial source of all things, he was filled with even more abundant piety, calling creatures, no matter how small, by the name of brother or sister, because he knew they had the same source as himself."[12] Bonaventure himself marveled at things both great and small, inviting us to consider

> The *magnitude* of things,
> in the mass of their
> length, width and depth...
> The *multitude* of things
> in their generic, specific and individual
> diversity...
> The *beauty* of things,
> in the variety
> of light, shape and color
> in simple, mixed and even organic bodies
> such as heavenly bodies,
> and minerals (like stones and metals),
> and plants and animals –
> clearly proclaims the power, wisdom and goodness of God...
> therefore, open your eyes,
> alert the ears of your spirit, open your lips
> and apply your heart
> so that in all creatures you may
> see, hear, praise, love and worship, glorify and honor
> your God.[13]

Dominican Insights

Meister Eckhart (1260–1327) is one of the greatest exponents of paradox in the history of Christian spirituality. Cyprian Smith tells us:

> Eckhart keeps us perpetually swinging from one pole to the other; he will not let us rest in either. To rest in one and forget the other is to lose hold of the truth, which is essentially paradoxical. God is everything, but nothing; distinct from creation, yet indistinct from it; there is tension between action and contemplation, withdrawal and involvement, silence and speech, being and nothingness. Having made a statement Eckhart will often go on to deny it;

---

12. Cousins, *Bonaventure*, 254–55.
13. Cousins, *Bonaventure*, 65–67.

but the truth lies neither in the affirmation nor the denial, but in the tug-of-war between the two.[14]

It is the key to unlocking knowledge of God:

> This swinging rhythm or oscillation between unlike poles, breathing in and breathing out, speaking and remaining silent, doing and resting, is the basic rhythm of the spiritual life, and it is only within the rhythm that we can know God, experience God, think and talk about God. If we abandon ourselves to this rhythm, let ourselves be carried by it, it will gradually kindle with us the spark of Divine Knowledge.[15]

Eckhart invites us to discover the depths:

> Think of the soul as a vortex or a whirlpool
>   And you will understand how we are to
> Sink
>   eternally
>   from negation
>   to negation
>   into the one.
> And how we are to
> Sink
>   eternally
>   from letting go
>   to letting go
>   into God.[16]

For Eckhart, God is ever creative, constantly creating. Creation is the outgoing, overflowing ebullience and creativity of God in Christ, to be greeted in the theophanies of the heavens and earth, and in the deep, imaginative powers of the soul: "I have often said, God is creating the whole world now this instant. Everything God made six thousand years ago and more when He made this world, God is creating now all at once."[17] Rejecting pantheism but affirming panentheism, Eckhart encourages us to encounter, greet and serve the Cosmic Christ in every element of creation, at every moment.

---

14. Smith, *Paradox*, 27.
15. Smith, *Paradox*, 26.
16. Fox, *Meister Eckhart*, 49. For a useful anthology, see Fleming, *Meister Eckhart*.
17. Quoted in Woods, *Eckhart's Way*, 95.

3 RECENT AND CONTEMPORARY PERSPECTIVES

Pierre Teilhard de Chardin (1881–1955), controversial and groundbreaking scientist and Jesuit, had first encountered the desert in 1905 when he lived in Cairo for three years as part of his training for ordination. Later, de Chardin went into the deserts as a treasure-seeker. A skilled geologist and paleontologist, he sought to unearth early fossils and the first human remains. De Chardin's mission was to seek amidst the dust and rock, clues to early life. He was focussed on microscopic evidences, the tiny indicators of early life embedded in the strata. But deserts, with their distant horizons, were to be the environment enabling him to gain the widest perspectives and expansive understandings of Christ, world and self. He went from micro investigations to macro and mega vision, from the tiniest details of rocks to mind-expanding outlooks. The vast open desert landscapes gave de Chardin his true treasures—a spaciousness of soul and breadth of perception.

The emptiness of the desert led de Chardin to think of the fullness, the *pleroma*, that Christ brings: the void of the wilderness pointed him to the ultimate fulfilment and completion in Christ (Col 3:11). In the desert he was beckoned to leave behind conventional, routine thinking about God—"the well-worn caravan routes of humanity."[18] He was ready to quit the usual roads and risk untrodden paths. Just before he headed into China's Ordos Desert, he noted in his journal that the one prayer necessary for him was "That I may see."[19]

This prayer was answered. He became captivated by an all-encompassing sense of the cosmic Christ, existing in all things and sustaining all things. As he looked at the material world, his vision, his seeing, was inspired by Colossians 1:15–17. He came to see Christ present in all things, in all matter, and as the fundamental principle of unity in a fragmenting world. The desert was like an irresistible magnet drawing him into this mystery.[20]

---

18. de Chardin, *Hymn of the Universe*, 56.
19. King, *Teilhard's Mass*, 129.
20. de Chardin, *Prayer of the Universe*, 58.

Breakthrough on the Feast of the Transfiguration

6 August 1923

It was in the Ordos Desert in Inner Mongolia that de Chardin was inspired to compose his great work *Mass on the World*. On the Feast of the Transfiguration in 1923, he found himself alone at sunrise watching the sun spread its orange and red light across the horizon. He was deeply moved, humanly and religiously. What he most wanted to do in response was to celebrate mass, to somehow consecrate the whole world to God. But he had no altar, no bread, and no wine. So he resolved to make the world itself his altar and what was happening in the world the bread and the wine for his mass. The Transfiguration had a special place in his life: his grand vision was the Eucharist and the Sacred Heart of Christ being the radiating center of the universe. For Teilhard, the Transfiguration was a precursor of the Second Coming when Christ would bring the universe home to himself. Teilhard's transfiguring Eucharistic theology emerges from his cosmic Christology, where Jesus Christ is not only the carpenter of Nazareth but also "the Alpha and the Omega, the principle and the end, the foundation stone and the keystone, the Plenitude and the Plenifier. . .the one who consummates all things and gives them their consistence".[21] In his *Mass on the World* de Chardin meditates on the meaning of the Offertory in the Eucharist:

> Since once again, Lord—though this time not in the forests of the Aisne but in the steppes of Asia—I have neither bread, nor wine, nor altar, I will raise myself beyond these symbols, up to the pure majesty of the real itself; I, your priest, will make the whole earth my altar and on it will offer you all the labors and sufferings of the world.
>
> Over there, on the horizon, the sun has just touched with light the outermost fringe of the eastern sky. Once again, beneath this moving sheet of fire, the living surface of the earth wakes and trembles, and once again begins its fearful travail. I will place on my paten, O God, the harvest to be won by this renewal of labor. Into my chalice I shall pour all the sap which is to be pressed out this day from the earth's fruits.
>
> My paten and my chalice are the depths of a soul laid widely open to all the forces which in a moment will rise up from every corner of the earth and converge upon the Spirit. Grant me the

---

21. de Chardin, *Science and Christ*, 34–35; cf. Rev 22:13, Col 1:17.

remembrance and the mystic presence of all those whom the light is now awakening to the new day.

One by one, Lord, I see and I love all those whom you have given me to sustain and charm my life. One by one also I number all those who make up that other beloved family which has gradually surrounded me, its unity fashioned out of the most disparate elements, with affinities of the heart, of scientific research and of thought. And again one by one—more vaguely it is true, yet all-inclusively—I call before me the whole vast anonymous army of living humanity; those who surround me and support me though I do not know them; those who come, and those who go; above all, those who in office, laboratory and factory, through their vision of truth or despite their error, truly believe in the progress of earthly reality and who today will take up again their impassioned pursuit of the light.

This restless multitude, confused or orderly, the immensity of which terrifies us; this ocean of humanity whose slow, monotonous wave-flows trouble the hearts even of those whose faith is most firm: it is to this deep that I thus desire all the fibers of my being should respond. All the things in the world to which this day will bring increase; all those that will diminish; all those too that will die: all of them, Lord, I try to gather into my arms, so as to hold them out to you in offering. This is the material of my sacrifice; the only material you desire.

Once upon a time people took into your temple the first fruits of their harvests, the flower of their flocks. But the offering you really want, the offering you mysteriously need every day to appease your hunger, to slake your thirst is nothing less than the growth of the world borne ever onwards in the stream of universal becoming.

Receive, O Lord, this all-embracing host which your whole creation, moved by your magnetism, offers you at this dawn of a new day.

This bread, our toil, is of itself, I know, but an immense fragmentation; this wine, our pain, is no more, I know, than a draught that dissolves. Yet in the very depths of this formless mass you have implanted—and this I am sure of, for I sense it—a desire, irresistible, hallowing, which makes us cry out, believer and unbeliever alike: "Lord, make us one."

On the feast of the Transfiguration de Teilhard recognizes that what is surrendered to God in the elements of the Eucharist is nothing less than the whole created order—not only hopes and pains of humanity, but also the desert, the forest, rivers and seas of the planet—every atom. The Host represents the round globe of the entire world. The Eucharist, in its epiclesis, will now call down the Holy Spirit on this offered universe, that, in the mystery of the Eucharistic consecration, the labors and pain of the world, every element within creation, might be suffused with the presence of Christ. As the Word Incarnate he is the cosmic Christ filling all things. Now, to encounter the rock or sand of the desert, to witness human achievement and loss, is to touch the very Divine. The universe has become the body of Christ, the flesh of God.

Inspired by Paul's vision "that God may be all in all" (1Cor 15:28), de Chardin believed that the world was in a state of continuous evolution, understood as the divinization of the universe. All life has become transfigured, transformed: the entire world has become sacrament, God-bearing, brimming with the divine presence. Now we can honor and respect God in all things. Now we can embrace suffering, knowing that, offered, it is filled with the Divine; we can embrace our daily toil knowing that God is in it. In the Transfiguration, aided by de Chardin's breadth of vision, we can allow our perceptions to be shifted, our understandings to enlarge. We can see things differently, and life may never be the same again. Fernández de la Gala observes:

> Teilhard dissolves old scholastic dichotomies. His theological vision seeks to harmonize a world convulsed by hatreds with the divine invitation to fraternal unity. He does so primarily by dissolving or discarding many of the Platonic dualities that church scholars never quite knew how to solve: body and soul, matter and spirit, the mud of the earthly reality and the angelic and celestial world.
>
> Teilhard, who considered himself a son of the ground more than a son of heaven, reconciles us with matter, proclaiming its natural goodness and its evolutionary mystery, and does not hesitate to give it the rank of sacredness, reminding us of the manifest acceptance of God contained in the Book of Genesis: "And God saw that it was good." He comes to call that divine acceptance "the hand of God and the flesh of Christ" by tangibly supporting God's presence in the world.[22]

---

22. de la Gala. "Teilhard de Chardin, consecration and the cosmos."

Discovering the Bigger Picture

The Transfiguration invites us to catch a glimpse of the bigger picture, the wider vision, the broader vista, which will give renewed meaning and purpose to our lives. We conclude with a look at two recent writers, who find in spirituality clues for a greater vision, moving from Jesus of Nazareth to the cosmic Christ.

Franciscan Ilia Delio ends her recent work *Christ in Evolution*: "Life in Christ can never be private or isolated, for Christ is the Word of the Father and the source of the Spirit. Christ is relational by definition and hence the source of community. To live Christ is to live community; to bear Christ in one's life is to become a source of healing love for the sake of community..."

Standing as a scientist and Christian within the tradition of de Chardin she concludes: "We must liberate Christ from a Western intellectual form that is logical, abstract, privatized and individualized... Christ is the power of God among us and within us, the fullness of the earth and of life in the universe... We can look forward toward that time when there will be one cosmic person uniting all persons, one cosmic humanity uniting all humanity, one Christ in whom God will be all in all."[23] How big is your vision? Is your God too small?

Contemporary spiritual writer Ronald Rolheiser recalls:

> Pierre Teilhard de Chardin was once called to Rome and asked to clarify certain issues in regards to his teachings. At one point, he was asked: "What are you trying to do?" His answer, in effect: "I am trying to write a Christology that is wide enough to incorporate Christ. Christ isn't just an anthropological phenomenon with significance for humanity, but Christ is also a cosmic event with significance for the planet."

He goes on:

> This concept challenges the imagination, implying far, far more than we normally dare think. Among other things, it tells us that Christ lies not just at the root of spirituality and morality, but at the base of physics, biology, chemistry, and cosmology as well. This has many implications:
> First of all, it means that the spiritual and the material, the moral and the physical, the mystical and the hormonal, and the

---

23. Delio, *Christ in Evolution*, 180.

religious and the pagan do not oppose each other but are part of one thing, one pattern, all infused by one and the same spirit, all drawn to the same end, with the same goodness and meaning. Simply put, the same force is responsible both for the law of gravity and the Sermon on the Mount and both are binding for the same reason.

All reality, be it spiritual, physical, moral, mathematical, mystical, or hormonal is made and shaped according to the one, same pattern and everything . . . is ultimately part of one and the same thing, the unfolding of creation as made in the image of Christ and as revealing the invisible God.

The fact that Christ is cosmic and that nature is shaped in his likeness means too that God's face is manifest everywhere. If physical creation is patterned on Christ, then we must search for God not just in our scriptures, in our saints, and in our churches. . . if Christ is also the pattern according to which the universe itself is unfolding, then what's good and what's inside of God is also somehow manifest in the raw energy, color, and beauty of the physical . . .

The famous, early Christian hymn in Ephesians speaks of "a plan to be carried out in the fullness of time to bring all things into one, in Christ." Christ is bigger than the historical churches, operates beyond the scope of historical Christianity, and has influences prior and beyond human history itself. It is Christ, visible and invisible—the person, the spirit, the power, and the mystery—who is drawing all things, physical and spiritual, natural and religious, non-Christian and Christian, into one . . .

Teilhard was right. We need a Christology wide enough to incorporate the whole Christ and our imaginations need still to be stretched.[24]

To live a transfigured life is to give up on narrow views of Jesus the Christ. It is to open ourselves to the widest possible understandings of Christ which refuse to place a limit on the scope and extent of his grace. It is to release ourselves daringly into ever-expansive, uninhibited visions of the Divine, while appreciating the God of the smallest details.

---

24. Rolheiser, "The Cosmic Christ".

QUESTIONS FOR REFLECTION

1. How can we maintain an attentiveness to the local without becoming excessively parochial in outlook? On the other hand, how can we live in solidarity with suffering peoples in very different places across the globe, while remaining rooted in our own locale? What clues do you get from John's gospel?

2. How do you find yourself responding to this expansive view of Christ, celebrating his theophany in atom and galaxy?

3. What do you think are the implications for spiritual practice of an all-encompassing cosmic understanding of Christ? In what ways can a narrower and more historical focus lead to intense action at the local level or impede an appreciation of the vastness of the ecological issues that now face us?

4. How do you find yourself reacting to Rolheiser's take on the Cosmic Christ? In particular, what is it saying to you about vocation and mission?

5. In a divided and fragmenting world humanity's cry is "Lord, make us one." How has your experience of the Transfiguration enabled you to recognize the potential unity of the world?

PRAYER EXERCISE

Go outside and enjoy using your five senses to appreciate God's world.
First, look down.
Attend to the tiniest details:

- Listen carefully—to the sounds you can hear
- Look attentively—notice the features in plants, leaves, rocks, wood, seeds: watch, observe
- Touch—feel the different textures, patinas and surfaces of your environment—as Bonaventure suggested "pray with your fingertips"!
- Smell—become alert to different fragrances—or whiffs!—in the air
- Taste the air—or take a biscuit or piece of fruit to savor!

Secondly, look up.

Consider the vastness of the sky. Delight in the shapes and movements of the clouds as they scurry or drift across the firmament. Even better: gaze at the velvety blackness of a night sky studded with the diamonds of stars. Pray for a sense of awe as you think of the unlimited world-transcending presence of Christ.

End with the prayer for the feast of Christ the King:

> *Almighty ever-living God, it is your will to unite the entire universe*
> *under your beloved Son,*
> *Jesus Christ, the King of heaven and earth.*
> *Grant freedom to the whole of creation,*
> *and let it praise and serve your majesty for ever. Amen.*

Basilica of the Transfiguration

8

Trusting
Between Memory and Hope

As we live our lives in the present moment, paradoxically we are caught between past and future, between memory and hope, between time and eternity. The Transfiguration brings together remembrance and fulfillment, commemoration and eschatology, beginnings and consummations. In the Transfiguration the first advent meets the second advent, transforming nostalgia and fear into hope. Ancient figures from the past—Moses and Elijah—meet present-day disciples. The story also cautions us about clinging needlessly to the past: Peter wants to build his three tents as a memorial or preservative of the moment, like the booths constructed in the Feast of Tabernacles recalling the Israelites' era in the wilderness. For Peter this revealed a strategy of evasion—he would rather dwell in the past than face the challenges of the Cross in the future. The liminal summit of Tabor itself stands as an intersection between past and future—a venerable mountain with a long history, flourishing now with newness of life in its lush forests, pointing to the skies...

How do you view the past? Why study the past? We need a sense of history, a perspective on where we have come from, culturally and spiritually. But our pasts, individually and corporately, may be scarred and wounded. Sometimes we bear bitterness or regret within our soul. We can get bowed down by guilt or nostalgia about the past.

What comes into your mind when you contemplate the future? Do you become anxious when you think of climate change, nuclear warfare—or on a personal level about ageing or infirmity? Are you fearful of what is to come?

In this chapter we see how the Transfiguration helps us to live creatively within this paradox, living in thanksgiving regarding the past, living in hope and confidence in respect to the future, and dwelling fully present to today, and to what God is offering us!

Between Sinai and Zion

In his study *Jesus on the Mountain* Terence Donaldson claims that the six mountains mentioned by Matthew point us to the past and to the future. They are not only a literary device, bringing structure to the gospel, but a significant theological symbol, with strong echoes from the Old Testament, appreciated by his Jewish Christian readership. He observes that whenever Jesus is on a mountain there is a resonance with both Mount Sinai and Mount Zion. On each, including Tabor, there is a looking back to the primal, protological mountain of Sinai, where God appears in his theophany and gives the Law and Covenant to Moses—celebrating God's purposes in the past. But there is also a looking forward to God's purposes in the future, gospel mountains resonating with Mount Zion, the last mountain, the eschatological mountain and symbol of the End Time, when all peoples will gather in the New Age of the Kingdom, as is expressed in Isaiah and Hebrews:

> In days to come the mountain of the Lord's house
> shall be established as the highest of mountains,
> raised above the hills.
> All the nations shall stream to it. Many peoples shall come and say,
> "Come, go up to the mountain of the Lord,
> the house of the God of Jacob,
> that he may teach us his ways and that we may walk in his paths."
> For out of Zion shall go forth instruction,
> the word of the Lord from Jerusalem.
> He shall judge between the nations
> and shall arbitrate for many peoples;
> they shall beat their swords into plowshares,
> their spears into pruning hooks;
> nation shall not lift up sword against nation;
> nor shall they learn war any more. (Isa 2:1–4)

> You have not come to a mountain [Sinai] that can be touched, a blazing fire, darkness, gloom, a tempest, the sound of a trumpet, and a voice whose words made the hearers beg that not another word be spoken to them...You have come to Mount Zion, to the city of the living God, the heavenly Jerusalem, to innumerable angels in festal gathering, to the assembly of the firstborn who are enrolled in heaven, to God the judge of all, to the spirits of the righteous made perfect, to Jesus, the mediator of a new covenant...(Heb 12:18–24)

Donaldson's study alerts us to what we might discover on the mountains. It affirms that when we tread the gospel mountains in Matthew, we learn deeply about two things—we learn something about Christ, who appears on the crests as a figure of awesome authority, giving us insights into his divine sonship. And we learn something about ourselves, about the vocation and destiny of the Church—it is very significant that God's people are always on the mountain with Jesus—he is never there alone—an image of the eschatological gathering of the community. As we recall the past (Sinai) we glimpse the future (Zion).

From quite a different angle, Kallistos Ware reminds us that in the Orthodox Church

> The feast of the Transfiguration is not simply the commemoration of a past event in the life of Christ. Possessing an "eschatological" dimension, it is turned towards the future—towards the "splendor of the Resurrection" at the Last Day, towards the "beauty of the divine Kingdom" which all Christians hope eventually to enjoy.[1] The Transfiguration of Christ recalls and restores the beauty of the unfallen world; it shows us the glory and wonder of the material creation as God intended it to be. At the same time, however, Mount Tabor does not simply look back to the beginning, but it also looks forward to the end. It is not merely protological, but eschatological. As Saint Basil the Great affirms, the Transfiguration is the prelude and inauguration of Christ's second and glorious coming.[2]

So we see in this chapter how time meets eternity and the past embraces the future. Things often kept apart come together in the Transfiguration.

---

1. *Festal Menaion*, 63
2. Ware, "Safeguarding the Creation".

TRANSFIGURING LIFE

1 LIVE IN THANKSGIVING FOR THE PAST

Living at the foot of Mount Sinai, the seventh century abbot of the monastery Anastasius, in his great *Homily on the Transfiguration* encourages us to cherish a sense of salvation history—the unfolding purposes of God in which we detect continuities through change and foreshadowings of events. In Moses, Sinai meets Tabor:

> Moses was present [on Tabor], standing at the right of the right hand of the Most High, a traveler arriving quickly from afar. As once he had gazed upon the bush, speechless and entranced by the Lord's presence, so now he gazed again on a bush, living and green in the analogous fire of God's presence in ensouled flesh. So, as he comes close to it on Tabor, he no longer says, "I will cross over and see this great sight" [Exod 3:3]. Now he is crossing from the time of the Law, crossing from types, crossing from shadows—leaving Egypt behind, crossing the Red Sea, coming through the darkness, passing through desert places... passing by Jericho, leaving behind sacrifice, leaving behind blood, crossing through the slaughter of a bull...

Anastasius has Moses addressing Christ:

> Now I see you who truly are and who eternally are, who are with the Father—you who say on the mountain, "I am the one who is!" I see this great vision: you who have long lain divinely hidden from me, now revealed as God...
>
> You are the mediator of old and new—God of old, yet newly human! You are the one who once revealed your name, invisibly, on Mount Sinai, and now you are visibly revealed, transfigured on Mount Tabor. For you love to enlighten us, as the heavenly, exalted one from the eternal mountains...

And Anastasius permits Moses to exalt in a sense of both history and fulfilment, as he says to Christ:

> You are the one who was prefigured on Sinai, and are now witnessed to and proclaimed by God on Tabor as Son.
> You are the one who once came down in the bush, and who swallowed up Pharoah's power in the abyss;
> You are the one who gave the chance to breathe freely again to people journeying on foot across a waterless desert;
> You revealed a rock to be capable of changing from dry to wet and from wet to dry—for you constantly form and transform our lack

of form and shape for the better, by your unchanging power of transformation.
You came from above to humanize and raise to life the human nature that here had lost its humanity by sin, and to raise up the tent of Adam, who had fallen.
You are the new tent, planted in truth for all humanity through incorruptibility and immortality.
You are the true temple.
You are the genuine altar of atonement.
You are the incorruptible ark of the covenant.
You are the true paschal lamb.
Nothing in the world is more delightful to me than to see you, and to be filled with your glory, your beauty, your image, your light, your revealed presence—when your dwelling has been unveiled before men and women, which once you foreshadowed to me in Mystery [on Sinai].[3]

2 LIVE IN HOPE AND CONFIDENCE FOR THE FUTURE

The Orthodox liturgies for the feast of the Transfiguration joyously celebrate on Tabor a foretaste of the Kingdom and a sign of the Resurrection:

> From love of mankind and in Your sovereign might,
> Your desire it was to show them the splendor of the Resurrection:
> Grant that we too in peace may be counted worthy of this splendor, O God,
> For You are merciful and love mankind.
> Prefiguring, O Christ our God, Your Resurrection
> You have taken with You in Your ascent upon Mount Tabor Your three disciples.
> When You were transfigured, O Savior, Mount Tabor was covered with light.[4]

Moreover, the texts also delight in how the event is a proleptic anticipation of the Parousia, the Second Coming:

> You were transfigured upon Mount Tabor,
> showing the exchange mortals will make with Your Glory
> at Your second and fearful coming, O Savior.[5]

---

3. Daley, *Light on the Mountain*, 171–73.
4. *Festal Menaion*, 470, 471.
5. *Festal Menaion*, 478. Texts modernized.

> On Mount Tabor the apostles, struck with wonder,
> trembled with fear before the beauty of the divine Kingdom,
> and they cried aloud:
> "Blessed are You, O Lord our God, for evermore."[6]
> To show plainly how, at Your mysterious second coming,
> You will appear as the Most High God
> standing in the midst of gods.
> On Mount Tabor You have shone in fashion past words
> upon the apostles and upon Moses and Elijah.
> Come and hearken to me, O you peoples:
> going up into the holy and heavenly mountain,
> let us stand in spirit in the city of the living God.[7]

Anastasius of Sinai sees Tabor revealing our very destiny:

> What is greater or more awe-inspiring than this: to see God in human form, his face shining like the sun and even more brightly than the sun, flashing with light, ceaselessly sending forth rays, radiating splendor? To see him raising his immaculate finger in the direction of his own face, pointing with it, and saying to those with him there: "So shall the just shine in the resurrection; so shall they be glorified, changed to reveal this form of mine, transfigured to this level of glory, stamped with this form, made like to this image, to this impress, to this light, to this blessedness, and becoming enthroned with me, the Son of God."[8]

Patristic commentators[9] take note of Luke's timing: "After eight days, Jesus took with him Peter and John and James and led them to a high mountain apart." They recognize great significance in the Eighth Day—for this was coming to be a symbol of the New Creation, an echo of the Greek idea of the *Ogdoad*: it represented the New Age, the Life of the World to Come. If the first seven days stand for the first creation—nature's making through six days and its sabbath—the Eighth Day stands for a new beginning, the age of glory and light, where evil has been forever defeated, and God reigns as all in all.

---

6. *Festal Menaion*, 490.

7. *Festal Menaion*, 494.

8. Daley, *Light on the Mountain*, 176.

9. For example John of Damascus and Anastasius of Antioch. Gregory Palamas later says the eighth day represents the coming age, an eternal day not measured in hours, never lengthening or shortening: Palamas, *Saving Work of Christ*, 41, 48

So, in his ascent up Tabor, Jesus is leading his disciples into the Kingdom of God, into the marvels and joys of the Eighth Day: the eschaton, the End which is also a new beginning for humanity and the cosmos.

3 LIVE FULLY ALERT TO TODAY

> Peter and his companions had been overcome by sleep, but becoming fully awake, they saw his glory (Luke 9:32, NABRE)

They could have missed it all. Like their drowsiness in Gethsemane, the three disciples succumb to sleep. We are discovering that the Transfiguration becomes an awakening in every sense. Once alert and responsive, they witness something never before told. Shaking off sleepiness to be able to encounter the new dawn of Christ, they anticipate Paul's exhortations:

> The night is far spent; the day is at hand. Let us therefore cast off the works of darkness, and let us put on the armor of light. (Rom 13:12, AV)

> Friends, you're not in the dark, so how could you be taken off guard by any of this? You're sons of Light, daughters of Day. We live under wide open skies and know where we stand. So let's not sleepwalk through life like those others. Let's keep our eyes open and be smart. People sleep at night and get drunk at night. But not us! Since we're creatures of Day, let's act like it. Walk out into the daylight sober, dressed up in faith, love, and the hope of salvation. (1 Thess 5:8, *Message*)

The Psalmist cries out to us: "O that today you would listen to his voice!" (Ps 95:7). As Hebrews 3:13 exhorts

> Help each other to stand firm in the faith every day, while it is still called "today", and beware that none of you becomes deaf and blind to God through the delusive glamour of sin. For we continue to share in all that Christ has for us so long as we steadily maintain until the end the trust with which we began. These words are still being said for our ears to hear: "Today, if you will hear his voice, do not harden your hearts as in the rebellion."

The Desert Fathers warn about spiritual sleepiness or drowsiness, which they call *accidie*—torpor, sluggish inactivity or inertia, lethargic indifference, depression. In the late fourth century Evagrius of Pontus characterizes it as "the most troublesome of all" of his list of eight negative thoughts.

His contemporary John Cassian depicted the restlessness of *acedia* as "the noonday demon": the monk "looks about anxiously this way and that, and sighs that none of the brethren come to see him, and often goes in and out of his cell, and frequently gazes up at the sun, as if it was too slow in setting, and so a kind of unreasonable confusion of mind takes possession of him like some foul darkness."[10] What is the answer to this prevalent condition?

Time Touches Eternity: The Sacrament of the Present Moment

In his great classic *Self-Abandonment to Divine Providence*, Jean-Pierre de Caussade (1675–1751) gives us the striking phrase "the sacrament of the present moment." He teaches us that we should not dwell in the past nor become anxious about the future, but rather transfigure the present by fostering an alert availability to God this very day and this very moment: "See, now is the acceptable time; see, now is the day of salvation" (2 Cor 6:2). Today, right now, God waits to meet us. De Caussade urges us to live in an attitude of continual surrender to God, yielding ourselves totally to him without qualification or preconditions, so we can become channels through which he can work: "Loving, we wish to be the instrument of his action so that his love can operate in and through us."[11] We are to live by humble trust in God, confident that he is working his purposes out. We are not to seek our own fulfilment but God's Kingdom: "Follow your path without a map, not knowing the way, and all will be revealed to you. Seek only God's kingdom and his justice through love and obedience, and all will be granted to you."[12] Abandoned into God's hands, we are to "go with the flow" as he opens and closes doors before us.

De Caussade encourages us to abide in a state of surrender to God. He urges his readers to strive for a synergy, an active co-operation with God's will: "We know that in all things God works for good for those who love him, who are called according to his purpose" (Rom 8:28). De Caussade believed that God is supremely active in the world, guiding all things according to his divine plans. Like the disciples atop Tabor, our part is to be awake and responsive to God's actions, to allow him to move and direct

---

10. Cassian, *Institutes*, 10:2. See Worssam, *In the Stillness*.

11. Muggeridge, *Sacrament*, 46. Caussade counters Quietism, which fostered passivity before God, withdrawal from the world, annihilation of the will, ending all human effort, to become totally available to God.

12. Muggeridge, *Sacrament*, 75.

our life in the midst of change. We are to train ourselves to recognize God's hand of providence in the "chances and changes of this mortal life."

De Caussade warns that we must not set bounds or limits to God's plans. He is a "God of surprises" working in unpredictable and unlikely ways, and we should be ready for anything: "The terrifying objects put in our way are nothing. They are only summoned to embellish our lives with glorious adventures."[13] Hardships can be in God's hands pathways to growth: "With God, the more we seem to loose, the more we gain. The more he takes from us materially, the more he gives spiritually."[14] We should not resent difficult circumstances, but rather listen to what God is saying to us through them.

How then is it possible to cultivate an attitude of such openness to God? De Caussade affirms that it is achieved by allowing Jesus Christ to dwell at the very center of our being. The Christ who longs to live within us is "noble, loving, free, serene, and fearless."[15] De Caussade has a vision of the Christ-life growing within each person who has the courage to surrender to him:

> The mysterious growth of Jesus Christ in our heart is the accomplishment of God's purpose, the fruit of his grace and divine will. This fruit forms, grows and ripens in the succession of our duties to the present which are continually being replenished by God, so that obeying them is always the best we can do. We must offer no resistance and abandon ourselves to his divine will in perfect trust.[16]

This is the secret of welcoming the fruit of "the sacrament of the present moment".

Wakefulness

The Orthodox tradition explores this in terms of *nepsis*—denoting wakefulness, attentiveness and vigilance:

> Watchfulness means to be *present where we are*—at this specific point in space, at this particular moment in time. All too often

---

13. Muggeridge, *Sacrament*, 40.
14. Muggeridge, *Sacrament*, 54.
15. Muggeridge, *Sacrament*, 109.
16. Muggeridge, *Sacrament*, 111.

we are scattered and dispersed; we are living, not with alertness in the present, but with nostalgia in the past, or with misgiving and wishful thinking in the future. While we are indeed required responsibly to plan for the future—for watchfulness is the opposite of fecklessness—we are to think about the future only so far as it depends upon the present moment. Anxiety over remote possibilities which lie altogether beyond our immediate control is sheer waste of our spiritual energies. A "neptic" person, then, is gathered into the *here* and the *now,* seizing the *kairos,* the decisive moment of opportunity.

As C. S. Lewis remarks in *The Screwtape Letters,* God wants us to attend chiefly to two things: "to eternity itself, and to that point of time which they call the Present. For the Present is the point at which time touches eternity. Of the present moment, and of it only, humans have an experience which God has of reality as a whole; in it alone freedom and actuality are offered them."

In the words of Paul Evdokimov: "The hour through which you are at present passing, the person whom you meet here and now, the task on which you are engaged at this very moment—these are always the most important in your whole life." He makes his own the motto written on Ruskin's coat of arms: *Today, today, today.* "There is a voice which cries to us until our last breath, and it says: Be converted today" *(The Sayings of the Desert Fathers).*[17]

"The Kingdom of God Is Among You"

To live a transfigured life is to be caught up in the "now/ not yet" tension of the Kingdom of God. It is to have a sense of salvation history and how God's purposes have unfolded in the past, despite humanity's obstructions to the divine plan or *economy.* It is to doggedly hold onto a confidence that "God is working his purpose out". The Transfiguration equips us to live in hope, ever ready, at each moment, to welcome the transforming light of Christ into our very midst—and calls us to be ever watchful for signs of the Kingdom, today! We long for its complete fulfillment as we delight in signs of its presence even now.

---

17. Ware, *Orthodox Way,* 153.

QUESTIONS FOR REFLECTION

1. What fears, if any, arise in you as you think of the future?
2. How can you turn such anxieties into prayer and into action?
3. As Donaldson suggests, on the mountains of the gospel we learn about two things: something new about the identity and work of Jesus, and something fresh about our own identity and vocation too. What have you learned from the mountain of Tabor about Christ, and about yourself?
4. How do you react to these prayers:

   > As this day begins we remember that you are risen, therefore we look to the future with confidence.
   >
   > You are the sole master of the future: keep us from despair and the fear of what is to come.
   >
   > We are assailed by doubts, and weighed down by anxieties—release our hearts, to journey towards you with hope. (*Divine Office*)

5. "See, I will create new heavens and a new earth. The former things will not be remembered, nor will they come to mind" (Isa 65:17). In what ways might fostering hope require a forgetting?

PRAYER EXERCISE

Review the journey or pilgrimage of your life, celebrating your own "salvation history". On a piece of paper draw a personal "timeline". Draw a horizontal line and mark it into the decades of your life, and be ready to add mountains and troughs.

Recall the mountains you have climbed: above the line, note major events and transitions, including new jobs, house-moves, births and deaths, new ministries. Then recall the valleys you have entered: below the line, note how you felt at these moments of change. How did you experience God at these moments? Bring this to a close by giving thanks for God's providence in your life, and entrust your future odyssey to him.

Maybe you can dare to use the Methodist Covenant prayer

> *I am no longer my own but yours.*
> *Put me to what you will, rank me with whom you will;*

> *put me to doing, put me to suffering;*
> *let me be employed for you or laid aside for you,*
> *exalted for you or brought low for you;*
> *let me be full, let me be empty,*
> *let me have all things, let me have nothing;*
> *I freely and wholeheartedly yield all things to your pleasure and disposal.*
> *And now, glorious and blessèd God, Father, Son and Holy Spirit,*
> *you are mine and I am yours. So be it.*
> *And the covenant now made on earth, let it be ratified in heaven.*
> *Amen.*

Conclude with the hymn by Arthur C. Ainger

> *God is working this purpose out, as year succeeds to year;*
> *God is working this purpose out, and the time is drawing near;*
> *nearer and nearer draws the time, the time that shall surely be:*
> *when the earth shall be filled with the glory of God as the waters cover the sea.*

Hiroshima Bomb, Feast of the Transfiguration 1945

9

Engaging
Between Transfiguration and Disfiguration

WHAT POSSIBLE RELEVANCE CAN the Transfiguration have to our world scarred by many different forms of violence and abuse, personal and societal, a planet soured by war and division? Is it not an escape, a flight of fancy? An exotic, eccentric irrelevance? In actual fact, it is located in the very midst of a vortex and maelstrom between transformation and desecration. In fact, Mount Tabor rises in majesty amidst a blood-splattered landscape of conflict. The ground is saturated with anguish. Beauty—and brutality. Glory—and gore.

From its summit one can view Mount Gilboa opposite, evoking the cry of David at the slaughter of Saul: "How are the mighty fallen!" Echoing across the centuries is his lament for beloved Jonathan:

> You mountains of Gilboa,
>   let there be no dew or rain upon you,
>   nor bounteous fields!
> Jonathan lies slain upon your high places.
>   I am distressed for you, my brother Jonathan;
> greatly beloved were you to me;
>   your love to me was wonderful,
>   passing the love of women. (2 Sam 1:21,26)

One of the earliest references to Mount Tabor in the Bible is in the violent narrative retelling the striking female leader Deborah (Judg 4). She recognizes the strategic importance of the mountain, and makes it a vital stronghold and base in her struggle with Sisera. She murders him by driving a tent peg through his skull when he was asleep. Indeed, the ascent today to Tabor begins at the Bedouin village of Daburiyya, preserving the memory of Deborah and Barak.

Throughout its history Tabor has been a strategic hilltop, overlooking the wide Jezreel valley and commanding fine views of the Via Maris, the ancient route between Egypt and Assyria. But the Plain of Jezreel was not only an important trade route: it also a battlefield, witnessing much bloodshed and conflict, for example in the time of Ahab and Jezebel (2 Kgs 10:7,11).

At both ends of the valley, military strongholds kept watch from strategic mountains. To the west, Megiddo has from 3000BC up to recent times sought to hold domination over traders and invaders seeking entry into the valley: this is the Biblical *Armageddon*, marked by the fortifications of many successive powers. Mount Moreh broods over the eastern end of the plain: here Gideon assembled his army against the Midianites (Judg 7:1). The Romans built a formidable military installation on Beth Shean's high ground, looming over the route from the Jordan Valley.

Tabor itself finds itself half-way along the Plain of Jezreel, and Josephus tells us that the Romans established a garrison at its crest, on the site that King Solomon himself had fortified. In 614 AD, it was the site of the Battle of Mount Tabor during a war between the Byzantine Empire and the Persian Sassanid Empire. The Byzantines used Mount Tabor as a stronghold but were defeated by the Persians. Both the Muslims and Crusaders built imposing fortresses on the summit of the holy mountain as they sought to command control of the area: a deep defensive ditch encircles the top of Tabor to this day. As I write, the Plain of Jezreel echoes to the booms of Israeli fighter jets, enroute to Lebanon.

Meanwhile, Mount Hermon, the alternative site of the Transfiguration, is under military occupation today. On the top, in the United Nations buffer zone between Syrian and Israeli-occupied territories, sits the highest permanently manned UN position in the world, while the southern slopes of Mount Hermon extend to the Golan Heights, where the Israelis have built a ski resort! They call the mountain "the eyes of the nation" because its elevation makes it Israel's primary strategic early warning system.

Contexts

One thing that strikes the pilgrim to the Holy Land today is the discomforting, shocking juxtaposition between the holy and the unholy, the sublime and the ugly, the peace-filled and the violent. Sacred land becomes scarred and scared:

- The "Little town of Bethlehem" is suffocated behind a 30 meter separation barrier.
- The Church of the Nativity is a mile from the teeming Dheisheh refugee camp.
- The Jordan River baptismal site is in a heavily mined militarized zone.
- Pilgrims' singing of "O Sabbath rest by Galilee, O calm of hills above" is drowned out by the sonic booms of fighter jets scrambled for attacks on Lebanon.
- The silence of the Judean desert is shattered by the overhead screeching of miliary jets.
- Jacob's Well in ancient Shechem is a few yards away from the Balata refugee camp, one of the largest in the middle east. The priest of the church was murdered by a settler in 1979.
- On the Via Dolorosa in Jerusalem Israeli soldiers keep watch, fingers on the barrel. The Third Station of the Way of the Cross, where Jesus fell the first time, is marked by a military checkpoint.
- Beside the Roman road to Emmaus at Moza is a firing range for the practice of soldiers.
- On the beaches of Tel Aviv lounge sun-worshippers; just forty miles south, 17000 children have been killed in the last year; in the first month of the war alone, October 2023, 25000 tons of explosives were dropped on the Gaza Strip, equivalent to two nuclear bombs.[1]

So it should not surprise us that the light-filled awesome event of the Transfiguration finds itself both in a context of violence and in a raw juxtaposition with episodes about human suffering.

> Jesus said to them, "Truly I tell you, there are some standing here who will not taste death until they see that the kingdom of God

---

1. Israel's high bombing rate made possible by AI targeting system called *Habsora* (Hebrew for "The Gospel").

has come with power." Six days later, Jesus took with him Peter and James and John, and led them up a high mountain apart, by themselves. And he was transfigured before them. (Mark 9:1,2)

The clearest meaning of this is that the Transfiguration event is a demonstration and revelation of "the kingdom of God come with power", with the "some standing here" referring to Peter, John and James. On the mountain, amidst a setting of human conflict, we will glimpse something about the grace, beauty and transformational character of the Kingdom. We recognize something of the wholeness and healing it brings into a world marked by fragmentation and polarity. Indeed, the mountain proclaims: the Kingdom of God is about transfiguration, transformation! The mountain experience of transcendence fuels the struggle for true justice in the world. We encounter the Kingdom in times of prayer, but this only serves to equip us to "seek first the Kingdom of God" in the midst of daily life.

Innocent Victims of Violence

As we consider what Jesus and the disciples faced on their descent of Tabor, we are struck by the sheer violence and terror of the boy's suffering, as Mark vividly conveys it:

> Teacher, I brought you my son; he has a spirit that makes him unable to speak; and whenever it seizes him, it dashes him down; and he foams and grinds his teeth and becomes rigid...
> When the spirit saw him, immediately it threw the boy into convulsions, and he fell on the ground and rolled about, foaming at the mouth.
> From childhood it has often cast him into the fire and into the water, to destroy him...
> After crying out and convulsing him terribly, it came out. (Mark 9:14–29)

The boy becomes a symbol and representative of all victims of violence, of all who are oppressed, denigrated, put down. He stands for those who cannot speak, whose voices are not heard. Correspondingly, the story challenges us as to how we might respond to such desperate need in the world today. He is the child of Gaza, of Sudan, of Ukraine...

FROM THE HEIGHTS TO THE DEPTHS

Jesus' descent of Mount Tabor symbolizes his *kenosis*, his abasement and journey from heaven to earth, as celebrated in Philippians 2, culminating in the hope that "at the name of Jesus every knee should bend, in heaven and on earth and under the earth." But before that might happen, Jesus first has to enter both the depths of the earth and the underworld. First "he humbled himself and became obedient to the point of death—even death on a cross" (Phil 2:8). Lee puts it: "The one who is transfigured on the mountain is the one who is disfigured by anguish, pain and death on the cross. Jesus climbs the heights before he descends to the depths, the one as necessary as the other."[2]

One of the things that strikes pilgrims to the Holy Land is the frequency in which they are required to *go down* into caves. Many of the holy places are, in fact, caves. Within the landscape of the Holy Land, Mount Tabor not only points to other mounts, but also points to the depths. The pilgrim needs to descend underground into sacred caverns, and, in the subterranean mystery, finds God at work. These hidden chambers in the bowels of the earth turn out to be liminal places, thresholds of the Divine, locus of theophany. At Bethlehem, the focal point of pilgrimage is the cave of the nativity described by Justin Martyr in 160AD: "When the Child was born in Bethlehem, because there was nowhere to rest in that place, Joseph went into a cave very close to the village."[3] The most important cave for Christians is the cave of the Christ's burial and resurrection, preserved in the *edicule* ("little house") in the Church of the Resurrection, the Holy Sepulcher.[4]

Our God is a descending God. The writer of the Letter to the Ephesians has a big question:

> Each of us was given grace according to the measure of Christ's gift. Therefore it is said, "When he ascended on high he made captivity itself a captive; he gave gifts to his people." When it says, "He ascended", what does it mean but that he had also descended into the lower parts of the earth? (Eph 4:7–9).

Cosby writes of the descending God: "If God is going down and we are going up, it is obvious that we are going in different directions. . . We will be

---

2. Lee, *Transfiguration*, 126.
3. *Dialogue with Trypho the Jew.*
4. See Biddle, *Tomb of Christ.*

evading God and missing the whole purpose of our existence."[5] God enters the depths: the caves declare that God reaches down to the deepest human need. There is no dark corner, no recess of grief, no hidden fear, no gloom of bereavement, no abyss of despair, no emptiness, no depths of misery that God cannot enter and transform. "Out of the depths I have cried to you O Lord, hear my voice!" (Ps 130:1). The Apostles' Creed declares: "He descended into hell." All this is foreshadowed on the lower slopes of Tabor.

FIVE SIGNPOSTS FROM MOUNTAIN TO VALLEY

1 Encountering Majesty, Above and Below

Before the Transfiguration, Jesus hands are sticky with his own spittle, which he uses to anoint the eyes of a blind man (Mark 8:22–26).

After the Transfiguration, an innocent child's disfiguring suffering awaits Jesus and his disciples. Jesus, elevated and radiant and aglow in the purity of divine light, now reaches down to the child writhing, face contorted, and foaming in the dust and the filth of the street, dashed to the ground in convulsions.

Luke tells us about people's reaction to this healing at the foot of Tabor:

> And all were astonished at the majesty of God. (Luke 9:43)

On the mountaintop the disciples had been overawed at the display of God's majesty. Now, back down in the valley bottom they experienced the majesty anew. The majesty of God is not confined to the mountaintop. It is to be discovered in most unexpected places, in our very midst, down below.[6]

Precisely the same word for majesty *megaleiotes* is used by the eyewitness in 2 Peter 1:

> For we did not follow cleverly devised myths when we made known to you the power and coming of our Lord Jesus Christ, but we had been eyewitnesses of his majesty. For he received honor and glory from God the Father when that voice was conveyed to him by the Majestic Glory, saying, "This is my Son, my Beloved, with whom I am well pleased." We ourselves heard this voice come from heaven, while we were with him on the holy mountain. (2 Pet 1:16–18)

---

5. Cosby, *By Grace Transformed*, 31. For exploration of underground spirituality see Mayes, *Journey to the Centre*.

6. The Greek word Luke uses for "astonished" means thunderstruck, awed.

The word *megaleiotes* conveys a sense of something awe-inspiring and humbling, evoking reverence. What is happening at the foot of the mountain that inspires this reaction? Jesus is rejecting fatalism, banishing despondency and resignation about one's fate expressed in the despair of the parent: "I begged your disciples to cast it out, but they could not." The majesty is revealed in the dust of the street. He is opening up a new future.

2 Discovering Prayer Atop and Below

Majesty is not the only link between the mountaintop and the valley. Luke tells us: "He went on the mountain to pray. And while he was praying, the appearance of his face changed" (9:28,29). As he came down the mountain to enter into the fray of human suffering Mark puts these words on his lips: "This kind can come out only through prayer."

Prayer above—prayer below. Prayer leads to the vision of the Kingdom of God—whether glimpsed in radiant glory or in a writhing agonized child. Myers asks: "By introducing prayer at this stage of the narrative [it is Mark's first reference to prayer of the disciples], is not Mark trying to suggest that he understands it to be the practice of critical reflection upon the 'demons within'? Is not prayer the intensely personal struggle within each disciple, and among us collectively, to resist the despair and distractions that cause us to practice unbelief?"[7]

3 Mountain of Prayer Points to Mountain of Faith

As Jesus goes up the mountain to pray, the mountain is a symbol of reaching to heaven, of touching the transcendent. But now the mountain becomes paradoxical, again. Viewed from below, the mountain takes on a new meaning. It now comes to represent something that seems impossible, immovable, implacable—but faith can move mountains! Immediately after the descent from Tabor, in the midst of the pastoral crisis, Jesus wants to talk about mountains—moving!

> Then the disciples came to Jesus privately and said, "Why could we not cast the spirit out?" He said to them, "Because of your little faith. For truly I tell you, if you have faith the size of a mustard seed, you will say to this mountain [Tabor], 'Move from here to

---

7. Myers, *Binding the Strong Man*, 256.

there', and it will move; and nothing will be impossible for you."
(Matt 17:19–20)

The mountain of transcendence points to the mountain of human need. It equips us to face the massifs of human suffering with a faith that can shift them! Jesus shows us a path through failure—from now on, we will not be intimidated or threatened by big problems, but rather summon the faith and prayer to conquer them.

4 Foretaste of Resurrection in the Midst of Pain

We note too that, following the resurrection-type appearance[8] atop the mountain, the valley too gives us a foretaste of resurrection in the midst of suffering.

> The boy was like a corpse, so that most of them said, "He is dead." But Jesus took him by the hand and lifted him up, and he was able to stand. (Mark 9:26,27)

We are being trained to recognize signs and pointers to resurrection in the midst of the everyday.

5 Majesty faces Betrayal

> Jesus rebuked the unclean spirit, healed the boy, and gave him back to his father. And all were astounded at the majesty of God. While everyone was amazed at all that he was doing, he said to his disciples, "Let these words sink into your ears: The Son of Man is going to be betrayed into human hands." But they did not understand this saying; its meaning was concealed from them. (Luke 9:42–45)

Everything is cheek-by-jowl, interlinked: majesty atop the mountain and a different expression of majesty below; astonishment at the majesty leads to talk of exodus atop and betrayal below.

Disfiguration is not far from Transfiguration. Here below, in Jesus' experience and ours, the two seem to belong together. Divine light is not confined to the mountaintop—it shines out, unexpectedly, in the midst of

---

8. Bultmann regarded the Transfiguration as a misplaced resurrection story.

human brokenness and vulnerability, whenever we allow the Kingdom of God to touch us.

Where was Andrew?

We note that Andrew is missing from the Transfiguration narrative. From the two sets of fishermen brothers Andrew and Peter, James and John—Andrew is absent. He is with them when they approach Jesus on the Mount of Olives (Mark 13:3) but not with the three when they witness Jesus raise Jairus's daughter from the dead (Luke 8:49–56) or stay close to him while he prayed in Gethsemane (Matt 26:36–38). What was he doing meanwhile? Did he miss all the action?

He was doing what he was always doing, since he joined Jesus' band: on the look out for signs of the Kingdom, here below. The gospels tell us that Andrew was often noticing people and opportunities that others missed. He had an instinct, an awareness: "Andrew first found his brother Simon and said to him, 'We have found the Messiah'" (John 1:41). When by the lake the crowd were getting hungry "One of his disciples, Andrew, Simon Peter's brother, said to him, 'There is a boy here who has five barley loaves and two fish'" (John 6:8,9). He alone, it seems, notices the potential. When the Greeks were seeking Jesus in Jerusalem, "Philip went and told Andrew; then Andrew and Philip went and told Jesus" (John 12:22). Andrew shows us that climbing mountains is not always necessary: what is needful is a watchfulness for clues of the Kingdom in front of our faces, "hiding in plain sight"!

LOOKING INTO THE FACE OF JESUS

Two of the Transfiguration accounts invite us to look into the radiant beauty of the face of Jesus. Matthew tells us that on the holy mountain "His face shone like the sun"—a visage aglow with light. Luke observes: "And while he was praying, the appearance of his face changed."

The next time the gospels invite us to look into the face of Jesus is in the context of the impending crucifixion:

> When the days drew near for him to be taken up, he set his face to go to Jerusalem. . .
> The Samaritans did not receive him, because his face was set towards Jerusalem. (Luke 9:51,53)

> [In Gethsemane] He fell with his face to the ground and prayed, "My Father, if it is possible, may this cup be taken from me" (Matt 26:39, NIV).
>
> Then they spat in his face and struck him; and some slapped him. (Matt 26:67)

The accounts of the crucifixion echo the Suffering Servant Songs of Isaiah, holding up a strange mirror to the Transfiguration. On Calvary

> I gave my back to those who struck me,
>   and my cheeks to those who pulled out the beard;
> I did not hide my face from insult and spitting (Isa 50)
>   here were many who were appalled at him—
> his appearance was so disfigured beyond that of any human being
> and his form marred beyond human likeness (Isa 52, NIV)
>
> He had no form or majesty that we should look at him,
>   nothing in his appearance that we should desire him.
> He was despised and rejected by others;
>   a man of suffering and acquainted with infirmity;
> and as one from whom others hide their faces
>   he was despised, and we held him of no account. (Isa 53:2–3)

On Tabor his robes became brighter than any earthly fuller could make them: "his clothes became dazzling white, such as no one on earth could bleach them" (Mark 9:3). On Good Friday we recall the words of Isaiah:

> "Who is this that comes from Edom, from Bozrah in garments stained crimson?"
> "Why are your robes red, your garments like theirs who tread the wine press?"
> "I have trodden the wine press alone, and from the peoples no one was with me;
> I trod them in my anger and trampled them in my wrath;
> their juice spattered on my garments, and stained all my robes.
> The year for my redeeming work had come." (Isa 63:1–4)

And so we find ourselves singing

> O sacred head, surrounded By crown of piercing thorn!
> O bleeding head sore wounded So shamed and put to scorn!
> Thy beauty, long desired, Hath vanished from our sight:
> Thy pow'r is all expired, And quenched the light of light.

Bombaro sees paradox and parallel:

Here, on the mountain, is Jesus, revealed in glory;
there, on a hillside outside of Jerusalem, is "this same Jesus" (Acts 1:11) revealed in shame.

Here his clothes are shining white;
there, they have been stripped off, and soldiers have gambled for them.

Here on Tabor Christ is flanked by Moses and Elijah, Israel's greatest heroes;
there on the mount of Golgotha, he is flanked by criminals.

Here at the Transfiguration a bright cloud illuminates the scene;
there at Calvary darkness overshadows upon the land.

Here a voice from God declares that this is his wonderful Son;
there, a pagan soldier declares, in surprise that this really was God's Son.

The mountain-top explains the hill-top; the hill-top explains the mountain-top. We only really understand either of them when we see each side by side with the other. On the Cross of disfiguration and at the Mount of Transfiguration we find God in Christ ruling through grace, mercy, truth, peace, and love. The crucifixion of the Son of God is about being surprised by the power, love, and beauty of God.[9]

THE CROSS: BEHOLD GLORY

So let's not confine glimpses of glory to the mountaintop. John celebrates the theme of transfiguration by inviting us to see "glory" throughout his whole gospel. It is the visible radiance of the divine presence—a sign that God is powerfully at work: "the Word became flesh and lived among us, and we have seen his glory, the glory as of the Father's only Son, full of grace and truth" (John 1:14). How is this glory to be revealed? God's glory is manifested through "signs". What is most significant is that the glory of God in the signs emerges precisely at the point of acute human need.[10]

---

9. Bombaro, "Jesus' Transfiguration and Disfiguration".
10. Water into wine; healings of nobleman's son, lame man, blind man; feeding 5000; raising Lazarus.

John also invites us to see problems and even fatal illnesses as situations that are pregnant with the glory of God. Even of Lazarus' serious condition Jesus can say: "This illness does not lead to death; rather it is for God's glory" (11:4). Again, outside Lazarus' tomb Jesus says to Martha: "Did I not tell you that if you believed you would see the glory of God?" (11:40).

The glory of God is supremely and paradoxically to be revealed on the Cross. While other parts of the New Testament suggest that Jesus first suffers and then receives glory in the resurrection/ascension (Luke 24:26; Heb 2:9), John alone sees the crucifixion of Christ as the greatest moment of glorification. In the fourth gospel, Christ can say of his passion: "The hour has come for the Son of man to be glorified" (John 12:23; see also 7:39; 13:31; 17:1–5). Jesus approaches his death not as a disaster to be endured, but as a glory to be embraced, for the Cross is the moment of salvation. From the Cross flows forgiveness and hope—it is the greatest hour of God's revelation, the laying bare of his presence.

Greek pilgrims to Jerusalem declare: "We want to see Jesus" (12:21). He directs them to where they will most clearly see him: "When I am lifted up from the earth, I will draw all people to myself" (12:32). The Cross will be not so much an oblation as a revelation: crucifixion becomes glorification, abasement an enthronement. We will be invited to see in blood and water dripping from the pierced body of Christ, the very birth of the church (represented in mother and beloved disciple embracing at the foot of the Cross) and a sign of the sacraments (19:35 cf. 1 Jn 5:5–8). Jesus' prayer is: "Father, I desire that those also, whom you have given me, may be with me where I am, to see my glory, which you have given me because you loved me before the foundation of the world" (17:24).

Once again, it is all a matter of looking, of seeing at depth: John quotes the scripture (Zech 12:10): "They will look on the one whom they have pierced."

THE PARADOX OF JOYFUL SORROW

Living within the polarities of transfiguration and disfiguration we discover what Orthodox Christians call "joyful sorrow": abiding trust in the unfailing love of God in the midst of a fallen world. The gospel tells us: "In the world you will be sorrowful; but when I see you again, your heart will rejoice, and your joy no one will take from you" (John 16:20). Yet grieving and hopeful joy need to co-exist in our hurting world. Sander puts it:

> The commingling of sorrow and joy within a believer's heart remains a mystery and also one of the primary tenets of the Orthodox faith. One without the other, reveals a kind of theological incompleteness. Paul observes that we are "sorrowful, yet always rejoicing" (2 Cor 6:10). John Climacus, in his *Ladder of Divine Ascent*, gave it the term *charmolypi* meaning "joy-filled mourning"— a feeling that manifests itself in tears—not of despondency, but of repentance and hope. Isaac the Syrian refers to tears that come from neither "triumphant joy nor abject despair, but from a prayerful encounter with God." Joyful sorrow is a characteristic of the faithful who live with the expectation of resurrection.[11]

Seraphim of Sarov (1754–1833) expressed it like this:

> Bear sorrows for the sake of the Heavenly Kingdom. Without sorrows there is no salvation. The Kingdom of God awaits those who have patiently endured. Acquire peace, and thousands around you will be saved.

SEEING THE KINGDOM OF GOD COME WITH POWER

That was Jesus' promise, as we have seen. But is he only referring to the explosive power of the light-burst on Tabor? Might he also be pointing us to how the Kingdom of God comes in the power of compassion and self-sacrifice? For it is precisely in the context of the coming Kingdom that Jesus, Son of Man, teaches:

> When the Son of Man comes in his glory, he will sit on the throne of his glory... The king will say to those at his right hand, "Come, you that are blessed by my Father, inherit the Kingdom prepared for you from the foundation of the world; for I was hungry and you gave me food, I was thirsty and you gave me something to drink, I was a stranger and you welcomed me, I was naked and you gave me clothing, I was sick and you took care of me, I was in prison and you visited me...Truly I tell you, just as you did it to one of the least of these who are members of my family—these my brothers and sisters—you did it to me." (Matt 25:31–40)

As Jesus says in connection with deliverance: "But if it is by the finger of God that I cast out the demons, then the Kingdom of God has come to you" (Luke 11:20).

---

11. Sander, "The Gift of Tears".

CHALLENGE

We began this chapter identifying the juxtapositions in the Holy Land between glory and pain. On the Feast of the Transfiguration 6 August, in 1945 came the starkest juxtaposition between transfiguration and disfiguration, between two different expressions of cloud and dazzling light, as the world's first atomic bomb was detonated above the people of Hiroshima, in a mushroom cloud and blinding light—not radiating glory but the poison of radiation. The transfigured life is led between the paradox of transfiguring grace and disfiguring realities. Our challenge is to be an agent or witness bringing transfiguring grace into situations of disfigurement and dehumanization. We seek to unleash the power of the Kingdom of God in compassion and self-sacrifice!

COMMITMENT

This means that we will rule nothing out—that we will live each day in the expectation that we will see Jesus in "his distressing disguise of the poor."[12] We will not confine the sacred to special times and places. We will train ourselves to discern the features of Jesus in the faces of those who suffer. We will seek to encounter majesty and mystery on the mountaintop of prayer and worship, but we will also be ready to spot glimpses or intimations of majesty in the valley below. As we exult in sunsets and mountains, in waterfalls and opening flowers and creation's beauties, we know that—in Tennyson's phrase—nature is "red in tooth and claw."

We will begin each fresh day renewing our resolve to glimpse possibilities for transfiguration and to seize opportunities for transfiguration. We commit ourselves to respond to disfiguration with hope and faith. We will imitate Jesus' reaction to the epileptic writhing in the dust—responding with tender compassion and prayerfulness. John Dear puts it:

> Following Jesus today in a land of nuclear weapons, rampant racism, and widespread economic injustice means actively going against our culture of violence.
>
> - As the culture promotes violence, we promote Jesus' nonviolence.
> - As the culture calls for war, we call for Jesus' peace.

12. Phrase of Mother Teresa of Calcutta.

- As the culture supports racism, sexism, and classism, we demand Jesus' vision of equality, community and reconciliation.

- As the culture insists on vengeance and execution, we pray with Jesus for forgiveness and compassion.

- As the culture summons us to be successful, to make money, to have a career, to get to the top, and to be number one, we race in the opposite direction and go with Jesus into voluntary poverty, powerlessness, humility, suffering and death.

- Discipleship to Jesus, according to the Gospel, requires that we love our enemies, demand justice for the poor, seek liberation of the oppressed, visit the sick and the imprisoned . . . .create community, beat swords into ploughshares . . .

If we try to engage in these social practices, we will feel the sting of discipleship and the Gospel will come alive.[13]

Living in the empowering light of the Transfiguration, we can recommit ourselves to working for reconciliation in situations of conflict, playing a part however small.

Where possible we will model forgiveness in situations of hate.

We will campaign for those robbed of human rights, seeking their restored dignity.

We will see what we can do to support the abused or marginalized in our locality.

We will respond in some way or another to the needs of the refugee, those exiled or made homeless.

In words adapted from Leonardo Boff:

> The Transfiguration is a process that began with Jesus and will go on until it embraces all creation. Wherever an authentically human life is growing in the world, wherever justice is triumphing over the instincts of domination, wherever grace is winning out over the power of sin . . . wherever hope is resisting the lure of cynicism or despair, there the process of Transfiguration is being turned into a reality.[14]

To live a transfigured life, we must be ready to face suffering—but not in a spirit of resignation or fatalism. On the contrary, we greet it as a potential

---

13. Dear, *Jesus the Rebel*, 29.
14. Boff, *Way of the Cross—Way of Justice*.

arena of grace and commit ourselves to see how, into situations of pain, the Kingdom of God might break through.

QUESTIONS FOR REFLECTION

1. Have you experienced a glimpse of glory in unlikely, unexpected places? Where?
2. What key insights has this chapter opened up or underlined for you? What challenges emerge for you at this point in time?
3. How do you think the Holy Spirit works through our conscience / consciousness in relation to the issues of this chapter? What can you do, in the face of the world's anguish and pain?
4. How does the Orthodox concept of "joyful sorrow" resonate with your experience?
5. In the light of the Transfiguration, how do you respond to these words of Paul:

> Whatever we may have to go through now is less than nothing compared with the magnificent future God has planned for us. The whole creation is on tiptoe to see the wonderful sight of the sons and daughters of God coming into their own. The world of creation cannot as yet see reality, not because it chooses to be blind, but because in God's purpose it has been so limited—yet it has been given hope. And the hope is that in the end the whole of created life will be rescued from the tyranny of change and decay, and have its share in that magnificent liberty which can only belong to the children of God!
>
> At the present time all created life groans in a sort of universal travail. We who have a foretaste of the Spirit are in a state of painful tension, while we wait for that redemption of our bodies which will mean that at last we have realized our full dignity in him. We were saved by this hope, but in our moments of impatience let us remember that hope always means waiting for something that we haven't yet got. But if we hope for something we cannot see, then we must settle down to wait for it in patience. (Rom 8:18–25, Phillips)

How would *you* express your Christian hope?

PRAYER EXERCISE

Use your hands expressively in this prayer-time in four actions.

Begin by clenching your fists tight and holding them before you. Feel the tension and let these fists represent an anger or frustration that bothers you today, a situation in the world that you feel strongly about. Hold them before God in the solidarity of prayer and intercession.

Secondly, slowly open your down-turned palms and let go of the tension. Let it fall away from you to God. In this gesture give to God any negative feelings or stresses, feel them drip out of your fingertips, as it were. Surrender the situation to God's providence and sovereignty.

Thirdly, turn your hands upwards in a gesture of surrender to God and of receiving from God. Breathe in what God wants to give you right now—perhaps a reassurance that all will be well. Breathe in his empowering Spirit who will give you the courage for action.

Finally, take a look at your hands. Is there an action that God is calling you to make in relation to your initial concern? What should you do as a result of this—something bold, something risky or rebellious?

Recall 2 Timothy 1:7 : "God did not give us a spirit of cowardice, but rather a spirit of power and of love and of self-discipline."

End with the Serenity Prayer: "God grant me the serenity to accept the things I cannot change; courage to change the things I can; and wisdom to know the difference."

Transfiguration by Raphael, 1520

10

Dancing
Between Mystical and Prophetic

ONE OF THE FUNDAMENTAL paradoxes in the Christian life is the interplay between stillness and movement. Some people feel torn apart between the call of duty and the call to prayer. They find themselves constantly juggling competing commitments to family and work with the need for rest and renewal. This can be compounded by guilt or a sense of failure. We can make sense of life by compartmentalizing commitments, but this leads to the dichotomy of a "split spirituality" and a divided self, as we are pulled back and forth. How can we reconcile the mystical—time for silent receptive prayer—with the prophetic—speaking out and taking action? What light can the Transfiguration shine on this everyday paradox? We noted that the Transfiguration account itself is boxed in and bracketed by situations of acute human need, demanding the attention of Jesus.

Pilgrims ascending Tabor today encounter on the mountaintop two complementary traditions of spirituality which can help us regain a fresh perspective. Let us listen to these voices from the mount.

BENEDICTINE WITNESS

Tancred—the Italo-Norman leader of the First Crusade later made "Prince of Galilee"—installed Benedictine monks on Mount Tabor in 1099, the year the Crusaders conquered Jerusalem.

They were massacred and their buildings destroyed by Turkish attacks in 1113 but returned, building a new church and monastery now defended with a stout wall, which resisted Saladin's onslaught in 1183. But after the defeat of the Crusaders on the nearby Horns of Hattin in July 1187 their presence ended: a Muslim fortress built on the site of the Transfiguration occasioned the Fifth Crusade.

Pilgrims and visitors today can walk through the surviving Benedictine ruins, especially the enduring walls of the oratory, chapter room and refectory. The buildings testify to a vision of wholeness and balance, embodied in the very fabric of the monastery, evoking a sense of the original layout, for they represent diverse commitments held together within a unity of purpose:

- Church: time to pray
- Noviciate: time to learn
- Guest house: time to welcome others
- Infirmary: time to care
- Scriptorium /library: time to study
- Chapter house: time to consult together
- Kitchen and cellar, bakehouse and brewery: time to meet bodily needs
- Refectory: time to eat
- Almonry: time to give alms to the poor
- Calefactory /warming room: time to relax
- Gardens and fields: time to work
- Dormitory: time to sleep!

The whole layout with its competing commitments was arranged around a cloister or walkway—this connected everything and formed the passageway to the Church. Traditionally, a Benedictine cloister would have at its center a spring or well, reminding the monks that Christ, the source of living water, should be the font and the center of all activities, making sense of the whole. The vision is expressed in the motto "ora et labora"—work and prayer.[1]

---

1. de Waal, *Living with Contradiction*.

Benedict of Nursa (480–547) had discovered this vision of wholeness in his cave in Subiaco in Italy, where he formulated a rule to guide spiritual seekers in the sixth century: "Therefore we intend to establish a school for the Lord's service. In drawing up its regulations, we hope to set down nothing harsh, nothing burdensome. The good of all concerned, however, may prompt us to a little strictness in order to amend faults and to safeguard love" (Prologue 45–47).

The *Rule* can be approached as a supreme example of wisdom literature. This is suggested by its opening words: "Listen carefully, my son, to the master's instructions, and attend to them with the ear of your heart. This is advice from a father who loves you. . ."[2] In recent years, there have been fruitful encounters between the *Rule of Benedict* and family life[3], and between the text and the business world.[4] But how can a *Rule* one and a half thousand years old be relevant to Christian life in the 21st century? Chittister helpfully points out: "*Regula*, the word now translated to mean "rule", in the ancient sense meant "guidepost" or "railing", something to hang onto in the dark, something that points out the road, something that gives us support as we climb. The *Rule* of Benedict, in other words, is more wisdom than law."[5]

Benedict's Three Vows

The triple vows of the *Rule* practiced on Tabor suggest a framework in which to understand and make sense of the sometimes conflicting dynamics of Christian discipleship. We find ourselves caught between the pull of duty to others and the pull of developing the self, and the first two vows suggest a dialectic within which this tension can be not so much resolved, as held creatively.

Benedict's vow of **stability** commits the monk to stay with a particular community for life. It is the first of the vows, because it is about the total surrender of one's life to God, within the particular setting and context of a group of people. In a world where people are rushing around in ever greater degrees of mobility, this commitment invites us to reconsider a rootedness in the here and now, an attentiveness to the needs of a particular

---

2. Fry, *Rule of St Benedict*, Prologue 1.
3. Robinson, *Family Cloister*.
4. Skrabec, *Rule for Business Success*.
5. Chittister, *Wisdom Distilled from the Daily*, 7.

community, and firmly rejects the temptation that "the grass is greener elsewhere". The vow of *stabilitas* reminds us of the essentially incarnational nature of discipleship, and of the call to be fully present to a particular historical context. But this vow also calls us to consistency, to steadfastness, as Benedict puts it: "to persevere in stability" (58:9). It calls us to the rock of faithfulness and constancy in a sea of change and tempest of transition. In today's context, this vow is about not giving up, not giving way under the pressures which confront today's Christian, which include marginalization and loss of respect in society. It is about rediscovering God's *hesed* or steadfast love and faithfulness, expressed in Paul's affirmation: "I am sure that he who began a good work in you will bring it to completion" (Phil 1:6).

Yet the Biblical metaphors of "standing in the evil day" (Eph 6) or "remaining in the Vine" (John 15) need also to be in conversation with the dynamic language of movement and motion with which Benedict both begins and ends his *Rule*:

> Run while you have the light of life (Prologue 13)
> Run on the path of God's commandments (Prologue 49)
> Hasten towards your heavenly home (73:8)

And so the vow of *stabilitas* stands in tension with Benedict's second vow of **conversatio morum**, the conversion of life, which calls for constant growth and change. This is an echo of the NT call to *metanoia*, turning again to God, and resonates with Paul's resolve: "Reaching out to what is before" (Phil 3:13).

Such a commitment can be both liberating and unnerving. It invites us to let go of cherished and familiar ways of working, to be ready for risk-taking, open to experimental and provisional patterns of witness and ministry which emerge as Christendom dissolves and the Church discovers different ways of being, in a post-Christian, post-modern world.[6] It calls us to accept the need for life-long learning and continuous development. It requires of us both a thirst for fresh understanding of God's Word and world, and also a vulnerability, a lowering of self-protective barriers, to be open to the God of surprises.

The third vow, **obedience** has behind it the Latin verb "to listen". By the vow of obedience the monk undertakes to listen deeply to God, the fundamental conversation going on in our lives. As the Voice from heaven cries out: "Listen to him!" But how?

---

6. See Harvey, *Another City*.

First we learn to listen inwardly . . .

- To our own heart, our feelings and responses to God
- To the inner words of God: his whispers and intimations
- To the Word of God in Scripture to us

But we also learn to listen to what God is saying to us outwardly in

- the cries of the poor
- the screams of the oppressed
- the sobs of the broken-hearted
- the sighs of our culture
- the laughter in people's lives

As we move between contemplative and apostolic lives, we do not rule out where or when we might hear his Voice.

FRANCISCAN WITNESS

Today the visitor to Mount Tabor is welcomed into the sanctuary by members of the Franciscan order, which gained custodianship in 1631. The current church was completed in 1924: architect Antonio Barluzzi built on the ruins of an ancient Byzantine church and a 12th-century church of the Crusader period. Franciscans had first come to the Holy Land in about 1217.

Francis' Dilemma

Francis himself had wrestled over the question of the relationship between activity and stillness and found himself torn between the two, as Bonaventure relates in his biography. Francis agonizes:

> What do you think, brothers, what do you judge better? That I should spend my time in prayer, or that I should travel about preaching? . . . In prayer there seems to be a profit and an accumulation of graces, but in preaching a distribution of gifts already given from heaven.

He went on to rehearse the advantages of a life dedicated solely to prayer:

> In prayer there is a purification of interior affections and a uniting to the one, true and supreme good with an invigorating of virtue; in preaching, there is dust on our spiritual feet, distraction over many things and a relaxation of discipline.

Ultimately he sees the truth that proves to be decisive:

> There is one thing that seems to outweigh all these considerations before God, that is, the only begotten Son of God, who is the highest wisdom, came down from the bosom of the Father for the salvation of souls in order to instruct the world by his example and to speak the word of salvation to people . . . holding back for himself absolutely nothing that he could freely give for our salvation. And because we should do everything according to the pattern shown us in him . . . it seems more pleasing to God that I interrupt my quiet and go out to labor.[7]

According to *The Little Flowers of St Francis* Sister Clare and Brother Silvester, after a time of prayer, agree on the same advice to Francis: "Continue with your preaching, because God called you not for your sake alone but for the salvation of others."[8] However, for Francis, this was never going to be an "either/or" choice. In the course of his mission, he established hermitages and retreats, and his whole ministry was an ebb and flow of action and contemplation. He models an integration of prayer into service, an inter-penetration and cross-fertilization between the two: "his mystical experience, far from cutting him off from the world, always sent him right back into its most basic realities."[9] Francis knew that the presence of God was not only to be found in stillness and solitude, but also in despised leper and feared wolf.

Francis composed *A Rule for Hermitages* showing that he values solitude amidst activity. In this text Francis puts only one biblical text. It related to the Kingdom: "And let them seek first of all the Kingdom of God and his justice" (Matt 6:33). Thomas Merton observes:

> The importance of the document lies in the spirit which it exhales—a spirit of simplicity and charity which pervades even the life of solitary contemplation. It reconciles what seems at first sight irreconcilable. Here Francis has completely reconciled the life of

---

7. Bonaventure, "Major Legend of Saint Francis" in Armstrong et al, *Early Documents: Vol. 2*, 622.

8. Blaiklock & Keys, *Little Flowers*, 54.

9. Rotzetter et al, *Gospel Living*, 180.

> solitary prayer with warm and open fraternal love. Instead of detailing the austerities and penances which hermits must perform, the hours they must devote to prayer and so on, the saint simply communicates the atmosphere of love which is to form the ideal climate of prayer in the hermitage. The spirit of the eremitical life as seen by Francis is therefore cleansed of any taint of selfishness and individualism. Solitude is surrounded by fraternal care and is therefore solidly established in the life of the Order and of the Church. It is not an individualistic exploit in which the hermit by the power of his own asceticism gains a right to isolation from an elevation above others.[10]

Francis' life of witness culminated in the experience of receiving the stigmata on Mt Alverna: the very wounds of Christ appeared in his own feet, hands and side. But this was not a private ecstasy. Rather, Bonaventure tells us in his *Major Legend*, it led Francis to fresh engagement with those suffering leprosy. He continued to say to his brothers "Let us begin, brothers, to serve the Lord our God, for up to now we have done little." Bonaventure tells us: "He burned with a great desire to return to the humility he preached at the beginning; to nurse lepers as he did at the outset."[11] This encapsulates Francis' testimony: the experience of prayer enabled a life marked by reaching out to others.

Today, in addition to caring for many holy places in the land, the Franciscans are committed to pastoral care and education throughout the region. Franciscans are not only focused on their own spiritual lives; they are also deeply committed to social justice. From serving the poor to advocating for societal change, they seek to be "the salt of the earth" by responding to the social and moral issues of their time. Their dual commitment to prayer and service is underpinned by love of creation and simplicity of living, coupled with advocacy for the poor and marginalized.[12]

The two traditions atop Tabor, the Benedictine and the Franciscan, complement each other: Benedict needs Francis and Francis needs Benedict—a sense of stability and rootedness comes into dialogue with a spirituality of pilgrimage, of the journey, outer or inner. Benedict is not entirely stationary, nor Francis ever on the road. Both find in Jesus a healing of

---

10. Merton, *Contemplation*, 263, 264.

11. Bonaventure in Armstrong et al, *Early Documents, Vol. 2* , 640. See also Jordan, *Affair of the Heart*, 51,52.

12. Today Franciscans in Holy Land run schools, parishes and clinics, while Benedictines are well-known for their ministry of hospitality.

the divides. Both celebrate the interplay between stillness and movement, which we see in the ministry of Jesus.

PENDULUM OF ALTERNATING PRAYER AND ACTION

In Mark's gospel, the Twelve are chosen "to be with him and to be sent out" (3:14). They are to spend quality time in the presence of Jesus and then venture forth in their apostolate. Both Mark and Luke emphasize the role of prayer and silence in the example Jesus sets before the disciples, following the forty days of prayer, struggle and preparation in the desert prior to the start of his public ministry. In Mark chapter 1, a hectic twenty-four hours of ministry is followed by prayer before dawn in an *eremos* –lonely place (1:35): the time of prayer is both the conclusion of an intense period of ministry and the prelude to the next stage. This rhythm of prayer and activity is repeated in the disciples' experience, as they go to a place of retreat enabling rest and reflection after first incursions into ministry and giving an account to Jesus (Mark 6:30,31). After this retreat, another time of ministry (6:35–45) is followed by Christ's retirement into the hills for prayer at night (6:46): the pattern of intense activity and solitude is repeated.

Luke gives a similar picture. Jesus withdraws to the hills and prays through the night after a demanding period in which great crowds gathered for preaching and healing (Luke 6:12). After another time of intense ministry, there is further prayer which becomes the context for learning and questions: "Once when Jesus was praying alone, with only the disciples near him, he asked them, 'Who do the crowds say that I am?'" (9:18). This passage vividly highlights Jesus modelling solitude to the disciples and the thin line between teaching and prayer. As Dunn puts it, we should note "the degree to which Jesus provided a model to his disciples as a man of prayer...To be a disciple of Jesus was to pray as Jesus prayed."[13]

He must leave the lonely places—heartened, challenged, instructed, comforted and energized—to face the demands of ministry and the call of the Cross. This rhythm between withdrawal and engagement, this ebb and flow of prayer and ministry, is the key to the ministry of Jesus: but there is more.

---

13. Dunn, *Jesus Remembered*, 561.

TRANSFIGURING LIFE

CONTEMPLATIVES—IN ACTION

A Mystical Heart Beating in the Midst of Action

The greatest challenge is not to set aside alternating times for prayer and stillness and times for service. The greatest challenge is to bring a contemplative heart into the bustling center of ministry. Jesus models not only the ebb and flow of prayer and action, but also the ability to maintain a listening heart in the very maelstrom of ministry. Certainly he lives within a rhythm of withdrawal and engagement, but it is in the heat of fierce debate that he is able to say: "Very truly, I tell you, the Son can do nothing on his own but only what he sees his Father doing...The Father loves the Son and shows him all that he himself is doing" (John 5:19,20). He only does what he hears the Father telling him, in his listening prayer (John 5:19,20; 14:10).

While Jesus cherishes and safeguards times of aloneness, he also brings his stillness into the midst of the noisy world: his desert heart still pulsates within him. He moves with an attentive heart amidst a clamoring, demanding world. The Jesus of John's gospel can only share and reveal what he himself has heard from his Father: "He testifies to what he has seen and heard, yet no one accepts his testimony" (3:32). Jesus is emphatic: "the one who sent me is true, and I declare to the world what I have heard from him" (8:26). He describes himself as "a man who has told you the truth that I heard from God" (8:40). He is clear: "the word that you hear is not mine, but is from the Father who sent me" (14:24). As he speaks, he is also listening! Here is a true healing of the dichotomy: not just an uneasy balance between silence and activity, between contemplation and action, but their very integration in the soul.

The Incarnate Life

Both the Franciscan and Benedictine ways practiced atop Tabor attempt to live out the Incarnation of Christ. They are expressions of what Melvyn Matthews calls "muddy mysticism"[14]—gritty grace—earthy dusty practical lifestyles concerned not only with heaven but also with issues of justice and care of creation. Again, the refrain echoes: "not either/or but both/and."

The Transfiguration event emerges as a healing, empowering force that brings into a unity the contradictions of the Christian life. The diverse

---

14. Matthews, *Rediscovering Holiness*.

elements are not brought together in an amalgamation, agglomeration or compromise but within an ongoing creative tension or dialectic that generates an energy and dynamic. In the Transfiguration Christ joins together everything that is set apart: he is a lodestone, a magnet. No longer is there any opposition or conflict between opposing forces. It is significant that the prayer-experience of the Transfiguration stands at the very center, the pivot of the gospel. Far from being marginal, it pulsates as the hidden heart of the drama of salvation.

Ultimately, it is the mystery of the Incarnation that makes sense of the oppositions between flesh and spirit, body and soul. In 451 the Church attempted to express the mystery out loud, affirming in the Chalcedonian definition:

> one and the same Christ, Son, Lord, only-begotten; acknowledged in two natures unconfusedly, unchangeably, indivisibly, inseparably; the difference of the natures being in no way removed because of the union, but rather the properties of each nature being preserved, and both concurring into one person and one hypostasis; not as though He were parted or divided into two persons, but one and the self-same Son and only-begotten God, Word, Lord, Jesus Christ.

This had been inspired by such texts as that by the writer to the Colossians:

> For in him all the fullness of God was pleased to dwell, and through him God was pleased to reconcile to himself all things, whether on earth or in heaven, by making peace through the blood of his Cross. (Col 1:20)

But we note: there can be no reconciliation between opposing elements without the Cross. The Transfiguration points us to the "exodus to be accomplished in Jerusalem"—the pivotal unifying event—the Cross. The Cross will truly be a journey into freedom, releasing us from the captivities of the past:

> For Christ is our living peace. He has made a unity of the conflicting elements of Jew and Gentile by breaking down the barrier which lay between us. By his sacrifice he removed the hostility of the Law, with all its commandments and rules, and made in himself out of the two, Jew and Gentile, one new humanity, thus producing peace. For he reconciled both to God by the sacrifice of one body on the Cross, and by this act made utterly irrelevant the antagonism between them. Then he came and told both you who

were far from God and us who were near that the war was over. And it is through him that both of us now can approach the Father in the one Spirit. (Eph 2:14–18, Phillips)

O faithful Cross, you stand unmoved, while ages run their course.
Foundation of the universe, creation's binding force.
(Stanbrook Abbey)

Franciscan Bonaventure Celebrates Paradoxes Healed in Christ

Reflecting on the Incarnation, **Bonaventure** anticipates the idea of the *coincidence of opposites*.[15] His great work *The Soul's Journey into God* embraces paradox as a vital part of the mystical ascent, leading the soul into the final stage of ecstatic contemplation. He invites us to contemplate the way that the two cherubim at each end of the Ark of the Covenant gaze at each other, as it were, across the divine space: it is as if the presence of God, represented in the stone tablets, brings together and unites the dualities of the world into a single mystery (Exod 25:20). He says that between the three Persons of the Holy Trinity

> Here is
> supreme communicability with individuality of persons,
> supreme consubstantiality [one single nature]
> with plurality of hypostases [different expressions]
> supreme configurability [bonding] with distinct personality...
> supreme mutual intimacy with [outgoing] mission...
>
> For the Cherubim who faced each other
> also signify this:
> the fact that they faced each other,
> with their faces turned toward the Mercy Seat
> is not without mystical meaning...
> for if you are the Cherub
> contemplating God's essential attributes,
> and if you are amazed
> because the divine Being is both
> first and last,
> eternal and most present,
> utterly simple and the greatest or boundless...

---

15. Nicholas of Cusa (1401–1464) established the term *coincidentia oppositorum*. See Cousins, "Coincidence of Opposites".

supremely one yet all-inclusive,
containing all things in himself –
if you are this Cherub,
look at the Mercy Seat and wonder
that in Christ there is joined
the First Principle with the last,
God with man, who was formed on the sixth day;
the eternal is joined with temporal humanity. . .
the most perfect and immense with the lowly,
the supreme and all-inclusive one
with a composite individual distinct from others,
that is, the man Jesus Christ. . .

When our mind contemplates
in Christ the Son of God,
who is the image of the invisible God by nature,
our humanity
so wonderfully exalted, so ineffably united,
when at the same time it sees united
the first and the last,
the highest and the lowest,
the circumference and the center,
the Alpha and the Omega,
the caused and the Cause,
The Creator and the creature,
it now reaches something perfect.[16]

Benedict would agree, in his own words:

Whether bond or free, we are all one in Christ.
The love of Christ must come before all else. . .
Pray for one's enemies in the love of Christ.
Hold nothing dearer than Christ.
Let all guests who arrive be received as Christ . . .
let Christ be adored in them as He is also received.
Prefer nothing whatever to Christ:
may He lead us all together to life everlasting.[17]

---

16. Cousins, *Bonaventure*, 105,107,108.
17. Fry, *Rule of St Benedict*, II;IV;V;LIII;LXXII.

JOIN IN THE DANCE!

To live a transfigured life we dance in the interplay between contemplation and action, between the mystical and the prophetic. In all our activities we seek to foster an inward stillness, an attentiveness to God in the very midst of movement. In the Transfiguration event, "Jesus came and put his hand on them. He said, 'Get up! Do not be afraid'" (Matt 17:7, NLV). Jesus is giving his disciples a hand-up, inviting them to walk with him and dance with him into the future. In fact, Jesus alludes to himself in the Gospel as the leader of a dance, both physical and metaphorical, asking: "But to what will I compare this generation? It is like children sitting in the marketplaces and calling to one another: 'We played the flute for you and you did not dance'" (Luke 7:32). I imagine Jesus also phrasing this positively: "The Kingdom is at hand. Listen to the children! As they are piping, they call out: 'come and join in the dance!'" In the Beatitudes Jesus says: "dance for joy, for surely your reward is great in heaven" (Luke 6:23).

In Christian theology, the dynamic relation between the persons of the Trinity was described by Basil the Great in the fourth century as a dance or *perichoresis*. This conveys something of the reciprocal, mutual indwelling of Father, Son and Holy Spirit. As the idea developed, it celebrated how humanity is called to participate in an ever-creative dance of the Trinity. The Trinity is not a dogma or idea, the Trinity is a dance to be joined! Baxter Kruger puts it:

> Before the universe came to be, before the heavens were called forth with stars and moons, before the earth was carved in infinite beauty and human life was fashioned with style and grace and glory, before there was anything, there was the great dance of life shared by the Father, Son and Spirit. In staggering and lavish love, this God determined to open the circle and share the Trinitarian life with others. As an act of mind-boggling and astounding philanthropy, the Father, Son and Spirit chose to create human beings and share the great dance with them.

The great dance becomes humanity's greatest paradox:

> In one way or another, aren't we all after the great dance? Is that not the story of our lives, our deepest longing? To my mind, the central passion of the human heart is to be filled with the great

dance, and the chief and maddening riddle of human life is to understand what the dance is and how to live in it.[18]

Henri Nouwen puts it: "That is the great and wonderful mystery of God becoming flesh to live among us. God invites us to learn to dance—not alone, but with others, sharing in God's own compassion, as we both give and receive it."[19] C. S. Lewis affirms:

> The most important difference between Christianity and all other religions is this: that in Christianity God is not a static thing—but a dynamic, pulsating activity, a life, almost a kind of drama, a kind of dance... The whole dance, or drama, or pattern of this three-Personal life is to be played out in each one of us: each one of us has got to enter that pattern, take our place in that dance. There is no other way to the happiness for which we are made.[20]

The musician John Fischer writes:

> The Spirit of God dances. He can't be tamed. He won't be contained. He refuses to be confined to a weekend retreat, an evening meeting, or even a moment of devotion... the Spirit of God dances out into the streets. He dances by the harlots in the red-light districts, by the victims of AIDS in lonely homes, by bag ladies in the inner cities... He finds the orphans and widows and dances through the lonely pain of their lives...

But is not only the Spirit of God who dances on the streets.

> Well, here I am. I'm out on the floor again and I can hear the music starting up. Great! I think I'm finally ready to dance. But wait a minute... this isn't a floor; it's asphalt. Good grief, we're out on the street! Oh no, I don't think I signed up for this. I thought this was going to be a nice, controlled Christian dance in the church hall... Somebody turned my nice, safe party out onto the streets... This isn't safe; this definitely is not safe. I thought this was going to be an entirely different dance.[21]

God leads our dance into the market places, where Jesus locates the children calling out to us. The Transfiguration catapults us out into the world of human need. Sydney Carter, author of the song *Lord of the Dance* tells us:

18. Kruger, *Great Dance*, 87,18.
19. Nouwen, *Turn My Mourning into Dancing*, 90.
20. Lewis, *Mere Christianity*, 148,149.
21. Fischer, *Real Christians Don't Dance!*, 123, 124, 119.

> I see Christ as the incarnation of the piper who is calling us. He dances that shape and pattern which is at the heart of our reality . . . I sing of the dancing pattern in the life and words of Jesus. Whether Jesus ever leaped in Galilee to the rhythm of a pipe or drum I do not know. Anyway, it's the sort of Christianity I believe in.[22]

> They cut me down
> And I leapt up high;
> I am the life
> That'll never, never die;
> I'll live in you
> If you'll live in me—
> I am the Lord
> Of the Dance, said he.
>   And I'll lead you all, wherever you may be,
>   And I'll lead you all in the Dance, said he.

PLUNGING INTO THE DYNAMIC OF GOD'S KINGDOM

The dance metaphor is one way of summing up the sense of dynamic and energy unleashed by the paradoxes of the Kingdom of God. The circle dance expresses the meeting of polarities, as participants draw together from different sides meeting in the center like opposing elements embracing each other, then step back again to the perimeter, respecting the Otherness of those opposite. Not a rugby scrum scrambling for control of the ball, but a graceful movement to and fro.

We've pondered how the Transfiguration is prefaced by the intriguing words: "Some who have taken their stand right here are going to see it happen, see with their own eyes the kingdom of God" (Luke 9:27, *Message*). In reflecting on the Transfiguration, we find ourselves drawn ever deeper into the "mysteries of the Kingdom."

Ultimately, we will indeed experience "the Kingdom of God come with power" to the extent that we risk opening ourselves to the grace of God who heals every dichotomy and invigorates paradoxes, turning them into springboards to a beckoning adventure. The Transfiguration empowers us and inspires us towards such an odyssey of the soul and courageous mission in a hurting world. The Transfiguration turns out to be a guiding

---

22. Carter, *Green Print for Song*.

lodestar, energizing tornado, mirror of truth, axis of beauty, matrix of healing and vortex of grace, epicenter of transformation—its centrifugal power radiating seismic implications for the universe, and its centripetal power drawing all things into Christ, the unifying center of all paradox. It emerges as the life-giving watershed and pulsing secret heart of the gospel—and of gospel living.

QUESTIONS FOR REFLECTION

1. How can we hold together the mountain and the valley *as one*—denying neither, and embracing both? What strikes you from the teaching of Benedict or Francis?

2. In what ways can you be "a contemplative in action"? How can we train ourselves to live daily life and commitments with a keener sense of attentiveness to the Divine in the mundane?

3. How do you find yourself responding to the idea of participating in God's universal dance of life—enjoying movement but somehow safeguarding an inner stillness?

4. How can you "practice the presence of God" in the everyday? What is your experience of living ordinary life in an atmosphere or climate of prayer?

5. In the Transfiguration narrative we've noticed how the disciples change

    - from apprehension to acceptance
    - from fearfulness to awe
    - from perplexity and puzzlement to wonder
    - from terror to trust
    - from sleepiness to wakefulness
    - from narrow thinking to expansiveness of vision

   As you review your journey through this book, can you name any shifts—in thinking or emotions—that have taken place within *you*? What might you want to do differently as a result of this book?

PRAYER EXERCISE

Make a review your life using the imagery of the mountain and the valley. How long each day do you allow yourself to linger on the mountaintop of prayer?

Reviewing the last 24 hours, what rhythm or balance of prayer and work have you managed? And a more difficult question: have you managed somehow to *integrate* reflection and a listening heart into the melee of the daily?

Or

Make a review of the rhythm of your life using the different elements incorporated into Benedict's monastery listed at the start of this chapter. What time—minutes or hours—do you give to each? Reflect—is anything out of kilter, creating a harmful imbalance? How can you fit all the elements together within your present lifestyle? Is there anything that needs to change?

End with

> It's good, Lord, to be here, your glory fills the night;
> your face and garments, like the sun, shine with unborrowed light.
>
> It's good, Lord, to be here, your beauty to behold
> where Moses and Elijah stand, your messengers of old.
>
> Fulfiller of the past! Promise of things to be,
> we hail your body glorified and our redemption see.
>
> Before we taste of death, we see your kingdom come;
> we gladly hold the vision bright and make this hill our home.
>
> It's good, Lord, to be here, yet we may not remain;
> but since you call us leave the Mount, come with us to the Plain.
> (J. Armitage Robinson, modernized)

Bibliography

Abhishiktananda (Henri Le Saux). *Saccidananda: A Christian Approach to Advatic Experience.* Delhi: ISPCK, 1974.
Alson, William P. *Perceiving God: The Epistemology of Religious Experience.* Ithaca: Cornell University Press, 1991.
Andreopoulos, Andreas. *Metamorphosis: The Transfiguration in Byzantine Theology and Iconography.* New York: St Vladimir's Seminary, 2005.
Armstrong, Regis J., Hellman, Wayne & Short, William J., eds. *Francis of Assisi Early Documents: Vol 2, The Founder.* New York: New City Press, 2000.
Aulen, Gustaf. *Christus Victor: An Historical Study of the Three Main Types of the Idea of the Atonement.* London: SPCK, 1970.
Barrois. Georges, tr. *The Fathers Speak.* New York: St Vladimir's Seminary, 1986.
Bartholomew, Ecumenical Patriarch. "Presentation to Metropolitan Nikitas". orth-transfiguration.org/resources/library/patriarch/presentation-metropolitan-nikitas/
Biddle, Martin. *The Tomb of Christ.* Thrupp, Stroud, Glouc: Sutton, 1999.
Blaiklock E.M. & Keys, A.C., trs. *The Little Flowers of St Francis.* London: Hodder & Stoughton, 1985.
Boff, Leonardo. *Way of the Cross—Way of Justice.* Eugene, Oregon: Wipf & Stock, 2021.
Bombaro, John. "Jesus' Transfiguration and Disfiguration". 1517.org
Borysenko, Joan. *A Woman's Journey to God.* New York: Riverhead, 2001.
Bowie, Fiona & Davies, Oliver, eds. *Hildegard of Bingen: An Anthology.* London: SPCK, 1990.
Carter, Sydney. *Green Print for Song.* London: Stainer & Bell, 1974.
Cassian, John. *The Institutes.* Trans. by Boniface Ramsey. New York: Paulist, 2000.
Chandler, Paul, ed. *A Journey with Elijah.* Rome: Carmelite Institute, 1991.
de Chardin, Pierre Teilhard. *Science and Christ.* London: Collins, 1968.
———.*Hymn of the Universe.* London: Fount, 1969.
———.*The Prayer of the Universe: Selected from Writings in Time of War.* London: Fontana, 1973.
Chittister, Joan. *Wisdom Distilled from the Daily: Living the Rule of St Benedict Today.* San Francisco: Harper, 1991.
Congregation for the Doctrine of the Faith. *Catechism of the Catholic Church.* London: Catholic Truth Society, 2012.

BIBLIOGRAPHY

Cosby, N. Gordon. *By Grace Transformed: Christianity for a New Millennium*. New York: Crossroad, 1998.

Craine, Renate. *Hildegard: Prophet of the Cosmic Christ*. New York: Crossroad, 1998.

Crossan, John Dominic. *Jesus: A Revolutionary Biography*. San Francisco: HarperCollins, 1994.

Cousins, Evert. "The Coincidence of Opposites in the Christology of Saint Bonaventure", *Franciscan Studies Vol.28* (1968), 27–45. St Bonaventure, New York: Franciscan Institute.

———.tr. *Bonaventure*. New York: Paulist, 1978.

Daley, Brian E., tr. *Light on the Mountain: Greek Patristic and Byzantine Homilies on the Transfiguration of the Lord*. New York: St Vladimir's Seminary, 2013.

Dear, John. *Jesus the Rebel: Bearer of God's Peace and Justice*. Lanham, MD: Sheed & Ward, 2000.

———.*Transfiguration: A Meditation on Transforming Ourselves and our World*. New York: Image/Doubleday, 2007.

Delio, Ilia. *Christ in Evolution*. New York: Orbis, 2008.

Donaldson, Terence L. *Jesus on the Mountain: A Study in Matthean Theology*. Sheffield: JSOT, 1985.

Dunn, James. *Jesus Remembered: Christianity in the Making*. Grand Rapids, Michigan: Eerdmans, 2003.

Dunn, James & McKnight, Scot, eds. *The Historical Jesus in Recent Research*. Winona Lake, Indiana: Eisenbrauns, 2005.

Fischer, John. *Real Christians Don't Dance!* London: Word, 1990.

Flanagan, Brian. "Jesus' Transfiguration". newwaysministry.org/2023/03/05/jesus-Transfiguration-what-a-queer- story

Fleming, Ursula, ed. *Meister Eckhart—the Man from Whom God Hid Nothing*. London: Collins/ Fount, 1988.

Fountoulis, Ioannes. "The Orthodox Celebration of Theophany." ocl.org/the-orthodox-celebration-of-theophany/.

Fox, Matthew, tr. *Meditations with Meister Eckhart*. Bear & Company, Rochester, Vermont, 1983.

———.*Hildegard of Bingen's Book of Divine Works*. Sante Fe, NM: Bear & Co., 1987.

———.*The Coming of the Cosmic Christ*. San Francisco, HarperOne, 1990.

Francis, Pope. *Evangelii Gaudium: The Joy of the Gospel*. Dublin: Veritas, 2013.

Freeman, Laurence. "Dangers of the Shallow End". *Church Times*, London, 3 July 2015.

Freyne, Sean. *Galilee, Jesus and the Gospels*. Minneapolis: Augsburg Fortress, 1988.

———.*Jesus, A Jewish Galilean: A New Reading of the Jesus-story*. London: T & T International, 2004.

Fröhlich, Gabriella. "Mondo X al Tabor". *Eco di Terrasanta*, 17 June 2008. terrasanta.net/2008/06/mondo-x-al-tabor

Fry, Timothy, ed. *The Rule of St Benedict in English*. Minnesota: Liturgical Press, 1982.

Gadamer, Hans-Georg. *Truth and Method*. New York: Crossroad, 1989.

de la Gala, Fernández. "Teilhard de Chardin, Consecration and the Cosmos: How a Jesuit Mystic Expanded the Scope of Theology". americamagazine.org

van Gennep, Arnold. *The Rites of Passage*. London: Routledge, 2010.

Gregory of Nyssa. *Life of Moses*.Trans.by Abraham J. Malherbe. New York: Paulist, 1978.

Haaretz, "Documents Reveal Israel's Intent to Forcibly Expel the Bedouin From Their Lands." haaretz.com/israel-news/2022-21-31/

Harries, Richard. "Meanings Scripture Alone Cannot Unfold". Church Times 6 December 2024.
Harvey, Barry A. *Another City: An Ecclesiological Primer for a Post-Christian World.* Harrisburg, Penn: Trinity, 1999.
Hauerwas, Stanley & Willimon, William. *Resident Aliens: Life in the Christian Colony.* Nashville, Tennessee: Abingdon, 2014.
Hengel, Martin. *The Charismatic Leader and his Followers.* Eugene, Oregon: Wipf & Stock, 1968.
Herbert, George. *The Complete English Works.* London: David Campbell, 1995.
Horsley, Richard. *Archaeology, History and Society.* New York: Continuum, 1996.
———.*Jesus and Empire: The Kingdom of God and the New World Disorder.* Minneapolis: Fortress, 2002.
Hughes, Gerald W. *God in All Things.* London: Hodder & Stoughton, 2003.
Hurtado, Larry W. and Owen, Paul L. *"Who is This Son of Man?" The Latest Scholarship on a Puzzling Expression of the Historical Jesus.* New York: T & T Clark, 2012.
Jewish Publication Society. *The Holy Scriptures According to the Masoretic Text: a New Translation.* Chicago: Lakeside, 1917.
Jordan, Pauline. *An Affair of the Heart: A Biblical and Franciscan Journey.* Leominster: Gracewing, 2008.
Kesolopoulos, Anestis G. *Man and the Environment: A Study of St Symeon, the New Theologian.* New York: St Vladimir's Seminary, 2001.
King, Thomas M. *Teilhard's Mass: Approaches to "The Mass on the World."* New York: Paulist, 2005.
Kruger, C. Baxter. *The Great Dance: The Christian Vision Revisited.* Vancouver: Regent College, 2005
Lee, Dorothy. *Transfiguration.* New York: Continuum, 2004.
Lee, Sang Hyun. *From a Liminal Place.* Minneapolis: Fortress, 2010.
Leech, Ken. *Soul Friend.* London: SPCK, 1997.
Lewis C. S. *Mere Christianity.* London: Fontana, 1955.
Liguori, Riccardo. "Father Eligio: His Experience in Rehabilitating Drug Addicts—The Caritas of Umbria and Tuscany meet the Mondo X community." La Voce, 31 May 2002. lavoce.it/padre-eligio-la-sua-esperienza-nel-recupero-dei-tossicodipendenti/
Lossky, Vladimir. *The Mystical Theology of the Eastern Church.* London: James Clarke, 1957.
———.*In the Image and Likeness of God.* New York: St Vladimir's Seminary, 2003.
Louth, Andrew. *The Origins of the Christian Mystical Tradition.* Oxford: Oxford University Press, 2007.
———.*Denys the Aeropagite.* New York: Continuum, 2002.
———."Theology, Contemplation and the University", *Studia Theologica* I, 2/2003, 64–73.
Macquarrie, John. *Two Worlds are Ours: An Introduction to Christian Mysticism.* Minneapolis: Fortress, 2005.
———.*Paths in Spirituality.* London: SCM, 1972.
Malina, Bruce J. *The New Testament World: Insights from Cultural Anthropology.* Louisville, John Knox, 1981.
Marsh, Michael K. "Thin Places, Veils, and Transfiguration". interruptingthesilence.com/2010/02/15/thin-places-veils-and-transfiguration

Matthews, Melvyn. *Rediscovering Holiness: The Search for the Sacred Today*. London: SPCK, 1996.
———.*Both Alike to Thee: The Retrieval of the Mystical Way*. London: SPCK, 2000.
Mayes, *Spirituality of Struggle: Pathways to Growth*. London: SPCK, 2002.
———.*Beyond the Edge*. London: SPCK, 2014.
———.*Journey to the Centre of the Soul*. Abingdon: BRF, 2017.
———.*Roads of Hurt and Hope: Transformative Journeys in the Holy Land*. Eugene, Oregon: Wipf & Stock, 2024.
McAfee Brown, Robert. *Spirituality and Liberation: Overcoming the Great Fallacy*. London: Hodder & Stoughton, 1988.
McGinn, Bernard. *Foundations of Mysticism*. London: SCM, 1992.
Meier, John P. *A Marginal Jew: Rethinking the Historical Jesus*. New York: Doubleday, 1991.
Merton, Thomas. *Contemplation in a World of Action*. London: George Allen & Unwin, 1971.
Meyendorff, Jean. *St. Gregory Palamas and Orthodox Spirituality*. New York: St Vladimir's Seminary,1974.
———. *Byzantine Theology: Historical Trends and Doctrinal Themes*. Oxford: Mowbray, 1975.
Miles, Margaret. *The Image and Practice of Holiness*. London: SCM, 1989.
Moltmann, Jurgen. *The Spirit of Life: An Universal Affirmation*. Minneapolis: Fortress, 2001.
Moses, A.D.A. *Matthew's Transfiguration Story and Jewish-Christian Controversy*. London: Continuum, 1996.
Muggeridge, Kitty, tr. *The Sacrament of the Present Moment: Jean-Pierre de Caussade*. London: Fount, 1996.
Müller, Mogens. *The Expression "Son of Man" and the Development of Christology: A History of Interpretation*. London: Equinox, 2008.
Mumford, Denise. *Martha, A Life of Dorothy Swayne, Lay Founder of TSSF*. Freeland: St Clare, 2014.
Musurillo, Herbert. trans. *From Glory to Glory: Texts from Gregory of Nyssa's Mystical Writings*. London: John Murray, 1962.
Myers, Ched. *Binding the Strong Man: A Political Reading of Mark's Sory of Jesus*. New York: Orbis, 2008.
Need, Stephen W. *Following Jesus in the Holy Land*. Durham: Sacristy, 2019.
Nouwen, Henri J. M. *Turn My Mourning Into Dancing: Moving through Hard Times with Hope*. Nashville TN: Thomas Nelson, 2001.
Orthodox Church in America. Department of Liturgical Music and Translations. oca.org/liturgics/service-texts
Palamas, Gregory. *Triads*. Trans. by Nicholas Gendle. London: SPCK, 1983.
———. "Sermon on Feast of Transfiguration". https://orthochristian.com/38767.html
———.*The Saving Work of Christ*. Ed. by Christopher Veniamin. Dalton, PA: Mount Thabor, 2023.
Palmer, George E.E., Sherrard, Philip & Ware, Kallistos, trs. *Philokalia, Vol 1, Vol 2*. London: Faber & Faber, 1981.
Palmer, Parker J. *The Promise of Paradox: A Celebration of Contradictions in the Christian Life*. San Francisco: Jossey Bass, 2008.
Peterson, Eugene H. *Christ Plays in Ten Thousand Places: A Conversation in Spiritual Theology*. London: Hodder & Stoughton, 2005.

BIBLIOGRAPHY

Pelikan, Jaroslav. *Jesus Through the Centuries*. New Haven: Yale University Press, 1985.

Pseudo-Dionysius. *The Complete Works*. Trans. by Colm Luibheid. New York: Paulist, 1987.

Ramsey, Michael. *The Glory of God and the Transfiguration of Christ*. London: Longmans, 1949.

Raya, Joseph. *Byzantine Liturgy*. Tournai, Belgium: Société Saint Jean l'Evangelist, 1958.

Rohr, Richard. *Everything Belongs: The Gift of Contemplative Prayer*. New York: Crossroad, 2003.

Rolheiser, Ronald. "The Cosmic Christ", ronrolheiser.com

Robinson, David. *The Family Cloister: Benedictine Wisdom for the Home*. New York: Crossroad, 2000.

Rossi, Andrew Vincent. "The Transfiguration of Creation". orth-transfiguration.org

Rotzetter, Anton, van Dijk, Willibrord-Christian, Matura, Thaddee. *Gospel Living: Francis of Assisi Yesterday and Today*. New York: Franciscan Institute, 1994.

Sander, Kurt. "The Gift of Tears: Some Perspectives on 'Joyful Sorrow' in Orthodox Art and Music". *Journal of the International Society for Orthodox Music* 2 (Nov 2016):90–96. journal.fi/jisocm/article/view/87810.

Savage, Sara et al, *Making Sense of Generation Y: The World View of 15–25 Year Olds*. London: Church House, 2006.

Scalia, Elizabeth. "Christ is baptized, not to be made holy by the water, but to make the water holy. . ." aleteia.org 2017/01/09

Schein, Bruce E. *Following the Way: The Setting of John's Gospel*. Minneapolis: Augsburg, 1980.

Schmemann, Alexander. *The World as Sacrament*. London: Darton, Longman & Todd, 1974.

Sheldrake, Phillip. *Befriending Our Desires*. London: Darton, Longman & Todd, 1994.

———. *Love Took My Hand: The Spirituality of George Herbert*. Darton, Longman & Todd, 2000.

———. *Images of Holiness: Explorations in Contemporary Spirituality*. London: Darton, Longman & Todd, 1987.

Silouan, Father. "Veiled Yet Unveiled, Open But Hidden." wisdomhermitage.org.uk/2019/10/17/veiled-yet-unveiled-open-but-hidden/

Skaltsis, Panagiostis. "Why Do We Bless Grapes For Feast of Transfiguration." johnsanidopoulos.com/2014/08/why-do-we-bless-grapes-for-feast-of.html

Skrabec, Quentin R. *St Benedict's Rule for Business Success*. Purdue: University Press, 2005.

Smith, Cyprian. *The Way of Paradox*. London: Collins, 1987.

Soelle, Dorothy. *The Inward Road and the Way Back*. London: Darton, Longman & Todd, 1978.

Stevenson, Kenneth. *Rooted in Detachment: Living the Transfiguration*. London: Darton, Longman & Todd, 2007.

Stăniloae, Dumitru. *The Experience of God: Revelation and Knowledge of the Triune God: Orthodox Dogmatic Theology*. Holy Cross Orthodox, 2005.

———. *Orthodox Spirituality*. New York: St Tikhon's Seminary, 2002.

Symeon the New Theologian. *On the Mystical Life—the Ethical Discourses (Vol 2: On Virtue and Christian Life)*. Trans. by Alexander Golitzin. St Vladimir's Seminary, 1996.

———. *The Discourses*. Trans. by C. J. De Catanzaro. New York: Paulist, 1980.

Tippett, Irena. "The Transfiguration by Theophanes the Greek". artway.eu

BIBLIOGRAPHY

Tobin, Frank, tr., *Mechthild of Magdeburg: The Flowing Light of the Godhead*. New York: Paulist, 1998.

Turner, Victor. *The Ritual Process: Structure and Antistructure*. Piscataway, New Jersey: Aldine Transaction, 1995.

———. & Turner, Edith. *Image and Pilgrimage in Christian Culture: Anthropological Perspectives*. New York: Columbia University Press, 1995.

Uhlein, Gabriele. *Meditations with Hildegard of Bingen*. Sante Fe, NM: Bear & Co., 1982.

Ulanov, Ann and Barry. *Primary Speech: A Psychology of Prayer*. Atlanta: John Knox, 1982.

de Waal, Esther. *Living with Contradiction: An Introduction to Benedictine Spirituality*. Norwich: Canterbury, 1989.

Vermes, Geza. *Jesus the Jew*. London: SCM, 2001.

Wallis, Jim. *The Soul of Politics*. London: Fount, 1994.

Walsh, John, tr. *The Cloud of Unknowing*. New York: Paulist, 1981.

Ware, Kallistos. *The Orthodox Way*. Oxford: Mowbrays, 1979.

———. *The Inner Kingdom*. New York: St Vladimir's Seminary, 2001.

———. "Safeguarding the Creation for Future Generations". Orthodox Fellowship of the Transfiguration. orth-transfiguration.org

Watts, Fraser and Williams, Mark. *The Psychology of Religious Knowing*. London: Chapman, 1988.

Wiederkehr, Macrina. *Seasons of Your Heart: Prayers and Reflections*. New York: Harper Collins, 1991.

Williams, Rowan. *Teresa of Avila*. London: Continuum, 1991.

———. *The Dwelling of the Light: Praying with the Icons of Christ*. Norwich: Canterbury, 2003.

Wolters, Clifton, tr. *The Cloud of Unknowing*. Harmondsworth: Penguin, 1976.

Woodruff, Sue. *Meditations with Mechtild of Magdeburg*. Sante Fe, NM: Bear & Co., 1982.

Woods, Richard. *Eckhart's Way*. London; Darton, Longman & Todd, 1986.

Worssam, Br. Nicholas. *In the Stillness Waiting: Christian Origins of the Prayer of the Heart*. Norwich: Canterbury, 2024.

Wrede, William. *The Messianic Secret in the Gospels*. London: James Clarke, 1971.

Zerwick, Max & Grosvenor, Mary, *A Grammatical Analysis of the Greek New Testament, Vol. 1*. Rome: Biblical Institute, 1974.